STEPPING UP
TAKING CHARGE
&LEADING THE WAY

A GUIDE FOR TEENAGE LEADERS

STEPPING UP
TAKING CHARGE
&LEADING THE WAY

A GUIDE FOR TEENAGE LEADERS

SHANE BARKER

BONNEVILLE BOOKS
SPRINGVILLE, UTAH

ISBN 13: 978-1-59955-503-4

Published by Bonneville Books, an imprint of Cedar Fort, Inc., 2373 W. 700 S., Springville, UT 84663
Distributed by Cedar Fort, Inc., www.cedarfort.com

LIBRARY OF CONGRESS CATALOGING-IN-PUBLICATION DATA

Barker, Shane R., author.
  Stepping up, taking charge, and leading the way / Shane Barker.
    pages cm
  ISBN 978-1-59955-503-4
  1. Church work with teenagers--Church of Jesus Christ of Latter-day
Saints. 2. Teenagers and adults--Religious aspects--Church of Jesus Christ
of Latter-day Saints. 3. Leadership--Religious aspects--Church of Jesus
Christ of Latter-day Saints. I. Title.
  BV4447.B26 2010
  259'.23088289332--dc22
                                    2010043150

Cover design by Danie Romrell
Cover design © 2011 by Lyle Mortimer
Edited and typeset by Kelley Konzak

Printed in the United States of America

10 9 8 7 6 5 4 3 2 1

Printed on acid-free paper

For Nathan, Amie, and Ashley

Other Books by Shane Barker

The Stripling Warrior Workout
Even the Prophet Started Out as a Deacon

Coming May 2011

I Thought Scout Uniforms Were Fireproof!

CONTENTS

CONTENTS

1

CATCHING TROUTZILLA

YOU CAN BE A TEENAGE LEADER

"CANNONBALL!"

Howling like a banshee, seventeen-year-old David James bounced off the diving board and crashed into the pool. Cold water blasted into the air, drenching people on the deck ten feet away.

David popped to the surface, his hair slicked back and a mile-wide grin on his face.

"Whoo-*hoo*!" he shouted. "Try to beat that!"

Responding to David's challenge, a freckle-faced deacon ran down the diving board. He bounced high off the end and flipped one and a quarter times before slapping onto the water in a teeth-jarring belly flop.

"Ow!" David winced and then shook the water from his head. "That's gonna be hard to beat!" David looked around and spotted a man standing beside a lifeguard tower.

"Bishop Souza!" he shouted, getting everyone's attention. "Bishop Souza next!"

The ward bishop tried blending into the background, but it was too late.

"Bishop, bishop, bishop," David chanted, encouraging everyone to join in. "Bishop, bishop, bishop . . ."

Knowing that escape was impossible, Bishop Souza finally walked to the diving board and—to an enthusiastic chorus of shouts and cheers—cannonballed into the pool.

The ward Young Men were celebrating after a long day of service projects. They'd spent the day mowing lawns, painting fences, picking up trash, stacking wood, cleaning garages, sweeping patios, cleaning gutters, and pulling weeds. As first assistant to the bishop in the priests quorum, David had been in charge. And though the day could have been long and boring, David had kept everyone entertained with a nonstop barrage of jokes, stories, and happy chatter. He'd kept everyone laughing and smiling, even though the work wasn't all that fun. His dynamic personality and contagious enthusiasm kept everyone in such high spirits that it hadn't seemed like work at all.

That wasn't the only time David's leadership had made a difference. Earlier in the summer, the Young Men had organized an Aaronic Priesthood encampment, and once again David had been in charge.

"We had 100 percent participation," he told me proudly. "Every deacon, teacher, and priest in the ward came . . . even those who don't normally attend a lot of Church activities."

How did he manage that? He started by visiting every teenage boy in the ward and convincing him he was needed. He had every single one believing the weekend would be a complete disaster unless he was there.

And he didn't stop there. David went the extra mile to make certain each young man had a great experience. He found ways to recognize every boy. He found ways to show off their skills and talents. He found ways for them to stand out.

For dinner the first night, for instance, David divided everyone into teams for what he called an "Iron Chef" competition.

"Every team had to cook something to contribute to our dinner," he explained. "And the bishopric judged the results."

David chose a young deacon to be his partner, deliberately choosing a young man who was especially shy and who had been reluctant to participate. Together they made individual fruit cobblers that they baked in orange peels in a bed of campfire coals.

"We didn't win first place," David said. "But we did win tastiest dessert . . . and everyone kept coming over to see what we were doing."

The result was that his young friend was suddenly the center of attention. And by the end of the campout, he went home not only feeling like a champion, but also feeling that he was a welcome, wanted, valuable member of the priesthood.

The weekend could have been filled with dull meetings and boring activities. But David made certain that everyone had a fantastic experience and that every young man went home feeling energized physically, mentally, and spiritually.

You probably know people like David. People who bring out the best in others. People who motivate, inspire, and energize their friends. People who can take charge and lead the way.

And you know what? You can be one of them.

I know a young woman who's the captain of her high school soccer team. Kylee is a gifted athlete who plays with the energy of a bottle rocket. But more than that, she uses her energy to drive the team, constantly encouraging and pumping up her teammates, bringing out the best in everyone around her.

"Go to the ball!" I heard her yelling during one game as she ran down the field. "That's the way! Good move, Natalie . . . now send it! *Send* it!"

Even when she was on the sidelines—when she was supposed to be resting—she still kept up a never-ending flurry of encouraging shouts and gestures. "Shoot, Mandy, shoot! Good job, Avalanche! Good job . . . keep the energy now. Ashley, go to the ball, *go to the ball!*"

Kylee is the driving force of the whole team. But the interesting thing is that she isn't the best player on the team. She's not the fastest, she's not the most talented, and she's not the most skilled. But she has so much enthusiasm—so much energy, drive, and charisma—that she sweeps everyone up with her momentum. She inspires everyone around her just by being there.

"She's like a spark plug," a player named Ashley told me. "We were practicing one day, and everyone was just kind of moping along, moving like robots and not having much fun."

"What about Kylee?"

"Kylee wasn't there. She had a scholarship interview that day and was late."

Ashley grinned. "But five minutes after she showed up, the whole team was sprinting around the field like we were on fire!"

I knew exactly what Ashley was talking about. I've known young leaders who've fired me up the same way. Haven't you?

Now you might be president of the deacons quorum. You might be a counselor in the Laurel presidency. You might be captain of the team, president of the club, or leader of the band.

Whatever the case, you have an opportunity to make a difference too. You have the power to point your group in the right direction and, like the engine of a fighter jet, blast them toward success.

Think you're too young? Think again!

The very fact that you're young means that you have an incredible advantage! You have energy, vitality, insights, and enthusiasm that older people often lack. You can blaze into action like a teenage whirlwind, energizing everyone in sight, sweeping them up with your momentum and inspiring them to elevate their game and lengthen their stride.

And make no mistake: the world *needs* young leaders.

Why? Because just as a coach can't get out on the field and play, adult leaders can't always get into the middle of the action either. But you can! You can get right out on the floor and take charge. You can inspire, encourage, and energize everyone around you. You just have to do it!

I used to spend my summers working at Boy Scout camps. One summer a boy named Jake worked on my nature staff. Jake was only fourteen, and he was small for his age, but he was one of the most gifted teachers.

One day he was teaching a fishing class. His students were rowdy fifteen- and sixteen-year-old Scouts who thought it was pretty funny having a "little kid" for a teacher. From the moment they laid eyes on him, they were determined to have as much fun as possible—and to make things as hard as they could for Jake.

But Jake wasn't intimidated.

"There's a huge fish in this lake," he told the bigger kids as he threaded a worm onto a hook. "I call him 'Troutzilla.'"

"How come you haven't caught him?" one of the bigger kids asked with a smirk.

"I have," Jake said, casually casting his worm far into the lake. "Four times . . . but I always let him go."

"*Riiiight*," one of the older Scouts responded, nudging a buddy with his elbow.

Jake just grinned. "Watch this," he said. "Ten . . . nine . . . eight . . . seven—oops! Here we go!"

Jake's pole bent wickedly as a hungry trout took the bait and sliced through the lake. Jake reeled his line skillfully, working the fish closer and closer to the bank until he could lift it carefully from the water.

"There," he said, showing off the fish to his stunned class. "*That's* what we're talking about!"

The older boys stood in shock, their eyes the size of pepperoni pizzas. Jake gently removed his hook and released the fish. He watched the trout shoot for deeper water and then turned to look at his spellbound students. "All right, then, you guys wanna give it a try?"

Did they ever! Five minutes earlier those older Scouts were too "cool" to listen to a younger, smaller boy. But now they were actually barraging him with questions.

"Jake, how do you get your worm to stay on the hook?"

"How does this look, Jake? Am I doing it right?"

"Hey, Jake . . . show me how you cast your line so far!"

Jake was more than a gifted teacher. He was an effective leader. Without being obnoxious or overbearing, he took command of his class, earned their respect, and got them *wanting* to know more.

The exciting thing is that you can do the same thing! You can work magic in your group just like David and Kylee and Jake. You can show your group how to snub mediocrity and rise to greatness. You can use your own strengths, talents, and enthusiasm to become an effective, dynamic leader. Really!

Many young people think it takes Harry Potter–like magic to be a good leader. But it really doesn't. With a few proven techniques and insights, you can be a leader who performs *real* magic. You can be a leader who performs miracles!

Let's try something. Get a pencil and try out the treasure hunt on the next two pages. Don't worry, it's not a test and you don't need to spend a lot of time on it. Just read each question and write down the first thing that comes to mind.

Are you ready? Go ahead.

LEADERSHIP TREASURE HUNT

1. Think of a great leader you've had. It doesn't matter if this person was an adult or someone your own age; just choose someone who had an impact on you. Write his or her name here:

_____

_____

2. What's one quality of his or hers that you'd like people to see in you?

_____

_____

_____

3. List three things you could do today to develop that quality:

_____

_____

_____

8. What can you do today to help your group achieve that? Now go do it!

_____

_____

_____

7. Imagine a newspaper writing a story about your group. What is the one thing you most hope they'd notice?

_____

_____

_____

6. Now list two things you can do today to help your group obtain that quality:

_____

_____

_____

5. Choose one quality you'd like your class or group to be known for:

_____

_____

_____

4. Think of a successful class, club, or group that you've been part of. What sort of things made it special or fun to be part of?

_____

_____

_____

Finished?

Okay, if you completed all the steps, you now have several good, solid ideas for getting started. You have things you can actually do today—things you can do right now!—to kick-start your group and send them *blazing* toward success.

But a word of caution: you have to do more than just read this stuff. You have to take action! You have to go out *today* and do at least one thing you listed in your treasure hunt. If you do, you'll see *instant* improvement in your skills and abilities.

And we're just getting started!

As you work through this book, you'll develop solid, energizing ideas for firing up your group. You'll learn to combine solid principles with your own unique gifts and talents to become a great leader—to become an *effective* leader. You'll learn to give people a glimpse of their own destiny and blast them toward excellence.

Are you ready to get started? Fantastic! Strap yourself in, and let's get to work!

ACTION STEPS!

- Think of some trait or quality you'd like people to see in you. (You might choose something like loyalty, for instance, or cheerfulness, endless energy, diligence, or stick-to-itiveness.) What is it? _____

  _____

- Think of one thing you can do *today* to develop that quality. Write it here: _____

  _____

  _____

  (Now be sure to follow through and actually *do it*!)

- Think of one skill, ability, or asset *you* have that an older person might not (such as enormous energy, wild enthusiasm, or outrageous creativity). Write it here: _____

- How can that quality help you as a leader?

  _____

  _____

  _____

- What's one thing you can do today to use that quality to improve your group? Write it here: _____

  _____

  _____

  _____

  (Be sure to follow through and go for it!)

- Think of at least one thing you can do *today* to make yourself a better leader. Write your ideas below. Not sure what to try? Then pick something from the following list:

  - Be more optimistic.
  - Smile more!
  - Give more compliments.
  - Find ways to boost and energize those around you.
  - Vow to never complain, whine, or groan.

  _____

  _____

  _____

- Find ways to recognize someone in the group who needs attention and then do something special for him or her. Describe here what you're going to do:

  _____

  _____

  _____

- Think of a great leader you've had. Now think of some quality *you* have that he or she didn't. Write it down here: _____

  _____

  _____

- Think of an effective teenage leader you've had. Explain why he or she was especially inspiring or effective: _____

  _____

  _____

- What can you do to develop those qualities yourself?

  _____

  _____

  _____

- Think of one thing you can do *today* to energize, motivate, or inspire your group. What is it?

  _____

  _____

  _____

Now . . . go do it!

2 THE GREAT PHOTO TREASURE HUNT
FORMING THE GROUP

"A BLACK DOG! We have to take a picture of a black dog!" Mandy Peterson looked up from her list. "Who in the ward has a black dog?"

"The Heatons!" someone exclaimed. "They've got a big dog!"

"It's a German Shepherd," someone else quickly pointed out. "It's not black."

"The Roberts!" a young woman named Talia shouted. "Their dog's black!"

"Come on!" Mandy yelled. "Let's go!"

The next second, the fourteen- and fifteen-year-old girls were dashing down the street toward the Roberts' home.

It was Wednesday evening, and the youth were competing in a photo treasure hunt. The Beehives, Mia Maids, and Laurels were racing against teams of deacons, teachers, and priests to take pictures of twenty-four items listed by the bishopric.

The rules were simple. Each group had to stay together as a class and they had to remain within ward boundaries. The first class to collect all twenty-four photographs would win.

And that was it. After the Mia Maids snapped a picture of the Roberts' dog, they dashed off to get pictures of bikes, trampolines, tree houses, and other objects scattered around the ward.

The deacons eventually won the contest (Mandy was certain they cheated, splitting up to get their pictures). But it was an energizing activity, and after enjoying punch and doughnuts, everyone went home excited and satisfied.

But there was more to it than that. The purpose of the race was to build unity and teamwork. It was to give each class a common goal, get everyone working together, and bond the groups together.

Which is a great idea. To launch your group onto a collision course with success, you've got to get everyone working together. You've got to get everyone helping, supporting, and trusting one another.

How do you do that?

There are three steps. First, you need to convince everyone that they're part of something special. Second, you need to get them moving in the same direction. And third, you need to convince each person that he or she is an important part of the team.

Sound tough? It's really not. In fact, it can be a lot of fun! Let me show you how to get started.

Make Them Part of Something Special

I happen to be a junior high school teacher, and I used to coach our seventh-grade football team. On game days, everyone on the team wore his jersey to school to remind his friends and teachers that they had a game that night. But more important, wearing those jerseys made the kids feel special. It let them stand out. It gave them a chance to show off and let everyone know they were part of the team.

I loved stepping into the hall on game days and seeing mobs of boys in maroon jerseys marching around together. The players hung out together before and after school, during lunch, and (when their teachers let them) even in their classes.

Why? Because people like to belong. They *need* to belong. They love being part of something special.

And your group can provide that sense of belonging.

Several years ago I coached a baseball team called the Bats. To this day, I can't tell you how many games we won or lost. But one thing I'll always remember—and the thing I'm most proud of—is that within a couple of weeks, those fourteen-year-old boys were more than just teammates. They were friends. Any time they were together, you could hear them planning trips to the water park, organizing pizza parties, or talking about going to the movies.

And it wasn't just the best players. Everyone was invited (even the little kid who didn't play very well). Those twelve boys bonded better than any group I've ever known.

Did it make a difference? You bet it did!

Whenever anyone struck out, he got nothing but support and encouragement back in the dugout. Whenever anyone muffed a play or dropped a fly ball, there was an instant chorus of players yelling, "It's okay," "Shake it off," "Forget it," or (this was my favorite), "Nobody's hurt! Nobody's hurt!"

And the little kid who didn't play very well? Two of the bigger, more athletic boys took him under their wings, working with him and giving him tips and pointers. And every time he made a good play, the whole team yelled and cheered and pounded him on the back like he'd just won the World Series.

Those kids were a *team*. They drew strength and energy from one another, forming a group that almost crackled with determination. And they made friendships that lasted long after our last ball game.

The question is, how do you get a team working together like that? Activities like Mandy's treasure hunt are a good start. Look for activities that get everyone working together, pursuing a common goal, and relying upon one another.

I have a friend named Ellen who belonged to her high school drill team. At the start of the year, the team went to an initiative course.

"It was crazy," she said. "There was an eight-foot wall, and we had to figure out a way to get all twenty of us up and over the top of it."

"How did you do *that*?"

"Believe me, it wasn't easy! And the instructors wouldn't give us any hints. They just kept telling us it was 'possible.'"

In the end, the girls formed a human ladder, climbing on one another's shoulders until they were able to reach the top of the wall. Then once they were over, they were able to reach back to give their teammates a hand up.

It took a while. But everyone learned the importance of working together, relying upon one another, helping one another, and trusting one another.

And that's what needs to happen in your group.

If you're stuck for an idea, try this: have everyone stand facing one another in a circle. Ask them to move in closely until everyone's pretty well scrunched together. Next, have everyone reach out with both hands, joining hands with two other people on the opposite side of the circle.

Everyone ready?

Okay, you've basically formed a huge, human knot. Without breaking the chain (releasing hands), the goal is to unravel the knot!

Seriously!

If everyone is careful—and patient—by lifting hands over people's heads and stepping over people's arms, you can eventually unravel the knot without anyone ever releasing hands.

It'll take a while! But everyone will *have* to work together. They'll *have* to cooperate. They'll *have* to make suggestions to one another, and they'll *have* to listen when others are talking.

They'll have to work as a team.

On top of that, bumping, jostling, and being so close to one another will break down many of the inhibitions people feel when they don't know everyone very well, which is a benefit by itself!

Try it! And make sure *everyone* participates!

Get Everyone Moving in the Same Direction

I once attended an air show at a local air force base. There were more than 200,000 visitors, which meant it was *crowded*. I wanted to look at a sleek fighter jet but got caught in a rush of people going in the opposite direction.

I tried working my way through them, but it was no use. Finally, I just gave up and "went with the flow." And the moving stream eventually got me where I wanted to go.

Now, imagine everyone in your group all going in different directions, working toward different goals and following different agendas.

Chaos!

But imagine if everyone was working together. Imagine everyone boosting, pushing, motivating, and helping one another to achieve the same goal.

It's a completely different story now, isn't it?

And is there any question which group would have the greatest chance of success?

If you've ever watched a bicycle race, you might have noticed that racers often ride extremely close together, one right behind the other. It's called drafting. As a cyclist races down the road, he creates a vacuum behind him. And if the second racer is close enough, that vacuum actually pulls him along. Drafting allows the second rider to race as fast as possible but without using as much energy. It actually lets him rest as he's speeding along!

When your group is racing along together, they're able to help one another just like that. By working together, they can accomplish more and with less effort.

Not only that, but the job will also be easier, and everyone will work better and have more fun too!

Make Everyone Feel Important

I was watching a marching band practice one day. Among all the drums and trumpets and saxophones was a young woman with a piccolo.

A *piccolo*!

Have you ever seen a piccolo? It's tiny! And as the band marched around the field, I wondered if anyone could actually hear the thing.

But as the band continued to march and play, I noticed something. That piccolo player was the person everyone else lined up with. She was at every key corner and at the end of every important line.

I still don't think anyone could hear her piccolo. But without her, the whole band would have been lost.

You need to remember that *every* member of your group is important. Every person can contribute something. To be an effective leader, you need to find ways for each person to contribute and to convince him that he's important.

Do this right now: Think of someone in your group who might feel unnoticed or unimportant. Now, can you think of a way to show him how much he's needed?

Could you give him a job? Put him in charge of something? Find a way to use a special talent or skill he might have? Think hard!

LEADERSHIP ACTION PLAN

Let everyone know they're an important, vital part of the group.

Make everyone feel as though they're part of something special.

Get everyone moving in the same direction.

When I was sixteen, I was assigned to home teach with an older man, and we taught two elderly couples. As we visited, the older folks would rattle on about different people they knew and how they were doing. Since I didn't know any of the people they were talking about, I'd sit patiently and wait for my turn to participate.

But after a couple of visits, my companion began drawing me into the conversation. He'd ask me to talk about the classes I was taking and how I was doing in them. He asked me to present lessons and to share my testimony, always going the extra mile to make me feel needed and important. He found ways for me to contribute so that I knew I was part of the team.

And that's the sort of thing you need to do in your group too.

If you've ever been part of a great group, you know what an awesome experience that can be. And you can provide that same experience for the members of *your* group. So let them know that they're part of something special. Get them all moving in the same direction, working toward the same goals. Give everyone chances to contribute so that each person knows he or she is an important part of the group. Then hang on and enjoy the ride!

ACTION STEPS!

- Find an activity that will bond your group together. It can be a game, a contest, a race against another group—anything that will get everyone working together, trusting one another, and relying upon one another. Write your idea here (if you're stuck for an idea, try looking up "initiative games" on the Internet or in the library): _____

  _____

- Choose a time to try your activity. Write the date and time here: _____

  (And be sure to follow through!)

- Think of one thing you'd like your group to be known for—something that would identify it as being special. What is it? _____

  _____

- What's one thing you could do *today* to get your group working toward that? _____

  _____

  _____

  Now go do it!

- Think of someone who might not believe he or she is an important part of the group. Write his or her name here: _____

- Now, think of something you can do *today* to let that person know that you care and that you're glad he or she is part of the group. Write your idea down here: _____

  _____

  _____

  (Be sure to follow through with your idea. Go out and do it *today*!)

- We'll discuss goals in a later chapter. But think of something your group could be working toward now, something that will get everyone moving in the same direction. What is it?

  _____

  _____

  _____

- What's something you can do today to get everyone started? _____

  _____

  _____

  (Do I need to remind you to actually go out and do it?)

- What can *you* do to get everyone excited about your plan? _____

  _____

  _____

Now go do it!

3
COLLISION IN THE RIVER!
COMMUNICATING EFFECTIVELY

FOR A SPLIT, TERRIFYING SECOND, I thought the boat was going to flip.

Shooting up from the trough, it rolled onto its side, tipping crazily, and then suddenly dropped and slammed straight into an enormous wave. Walls of icy water crashed over the bow, drenching everyone in the boat.

"Hang on!" Nick Daley shouted as the boat careened through the rapid. The tour guide clamped a hand onto his dripping safari hat. "Here we go again!"

The next instant the boat slammed into a monstrous wall of freezing water that poured over us like a waterfall.

I brushed the water out of my eyes and then jammed the throttle to the stops, sending the boat slicing through the churning waves. This was our second day on the Colorado River in the bottom of the Grand Canyon. The sun was hot and the air was dry, but the river water was so cold that every icy wave made everyone gasp for breath.

We were halfway through the rapid, and I was steering through the middle of the channel, when Nick turned frantically in the front of the boat.

"Left!" he shouted. "Left! *Left!*"

Even over the roar of the rapids, I could hear the urgency in his voice, and I didn't waste any time asking questions. I shoved the rudder hard to the side and hit the gas, driving the boat sharply to the left.

"Left!" Nick screamed, waving his arms. "Left! Le—"

The boat slammed into a submerged rock with a sickening *crunch*. I flew forward into the motor well, gashing my knee on the metal frame. I quickly regained my feet, grabbed for the rudder, and then steered the boat out of the maelstrom and back into calmer water.

Other than a four-inch gash on my knee (and a badly bruised ego), no one was hurt in the accident. But the submerged boulder snapped a chain beneath the boat and cracked the blade of our outboard motor.

"Why didn't you *listen* to me?" Nick asked later as we tried to repair the damage. I could tell he was pretty mad at me.

"I *did*," I said. "I was turning as hard as I could!"

"But you didn't lift the motor!" He held up the ruined propeller and shook his head. "If you'd lifted like I told you, we wouldn't have broken the prop."

"*Lift?*" I suddenly felt really stupid. "I thought you were yelling '*left!*'"

The whole thing seems funny now (and I still have a piece of broken chain on my desk as a reminder), but at the time it was pretty embarrassing. And it was all because of a mix-up in communication.

Few things will enhance your leadership skills as much as the ability to communicate effectively. After all, in order to get the job done right, you need to explain exactly what you need and when you need it. You need to explain exactly what needs to happen. And the better you can do that, the more effective you will be.

Not convinced?

Try this experiment: find a friend (or a handy brother or sister), and give him or her a piece of paper and a pencil. Turn around so you can't see what your friend is doing and then describe the figure on the following page, asking him or her to draw it. You can give any directions you want, just don't let the other person see it, and be sure not to peek at what he or she is drawing.

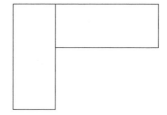

Finished?

All right, take a look at how you did.

The drawing turned out perfectly, right?

No?

If you're like most people, your friend's picture didn't turn out so well. And if you had trouble describing how to sketch a simple figure, imagine what might happen when you give directions for a more complicated project.

Are you starting to get the picture?

I was working as a ski patrolman once during a blinding snowstorm. A young girl had been injured on the hill, and a patroller named Matt skied off to help. The wind was howling, the snow was falling, and we were having trouble hearing Matt over the radio.

We were waiting for him to call us with the patient's vital signs and were shocked to hear him say, "No pulse!"

I was at the resort clinic at the bottom of the mountain, and we burst into action. I ran outside and fired up a snowmobile. A second later a doctor with a portable defibrillator jumped on behind me. I gunned the engine and shot into the storm. A girl's life was on the line, and I drove like a fighter pilot going for takeoff.

We roared up to the scene of the accident and found Matt talking calmly with his patient.

"Um, Matt," I said after we'd made sure everything was under control, "you told us she had no pulse."

Matt looked confused for a moment and then suddenly realized what had happened.

"No, no, *nooooooo*," he said, shaking his head. "What I *meant* was that she's wearing eight layers of clothes. I wasn't able to *take* her pulse!"

Stories like that are always embarrassing, of course. But they

23

happen to everyone. The important thing is to make sure they never ruin an activity of yours. So let's look at a couple of ideas.

Be Sure Everyone Knows What's Going On

A college student told me that before she joined the Church, one of her Mormon friends invited her to a stake fireside.

"Sure," Jennifer replied. "Why not?"

Jennifer sat politely through the meeting, but when it came time for refreshments, she became confused.

"Cookies?" she asked. "I thought we were having steaks."

"Steaks?"

Jennifer shrugged. "You did say this was a *steak* fireside, didn't you?"

To be an effective leader you need to make certain everyone knows what's going on. You need to make sure everyone knows what you're doing and what you're trying to accomplish. You'll find that everyone will do better if they know exactly what the finished product is supposed to be.

My friend Malia told me that at girls' camp, her ward was asked to remove a number of rotting benches from the amphitheater so they could be replaced. The problem was that several young women came late. They saw what everyone was doing and assumed they were replacing everything. By the time someone noticed what they were doing, the girls had removed *all* the benches—even the good ones, which then had to be collected and returned.

But my favorite story is about a Boy Scout who was assigned to make dinner on an overnight campout. One of the older Scouts told him that if he put soap on the bottom of the cook pots, they'd be easier to clean.

Unfortunately, the young Scout thought he meant the *inside* of the pot and, wanting the pots to be as easy to clean as possible, gave them all a good, thick coat.

I'll spare you all the resulting details, but just know the entire troop had one *miserable* night!

I'm sure you know how frustrating it is when you're participating in an activity but don't know what's going on. So keep everyone informed. Let everyone know exactly what's happening.

A few years ago I flew a small airplane to Brigham City, Utah. Brigham City doesn't have a control tower, so pilots keep track of one another by broadcasting their positions over the radio.

As I neared the airport, I heard a pilot radio that he was entering the traffic pattern. "Brigham City traffic," he said, "Seven Two Kilo is turning left downwind of Runway 34, touch and go."

Okay, I thought, looking ahead. *There's an airplane circling the airport, practicing takeoffs and landings. Gotta watch out for him.*

A second later, the pilot radioed back in a frantic voice.

"Brigham City traffic, be advised of a Piper Cub in the pattern without a radio. Maybe he's on the wrong frequency or something, but he's not broadcasting, and he's buzzing around like he owns the place!"

Uh-oh, I thought, peering into the distance. A moment later I spotted the wayward pilot. I was able to keep out of his way because another pilot had told me what was going on.

As a leader, be sure everyone in your group *always* knows what's going on too.

Be Sure Everyone Knows What You Expect

One year the drama department at my junior high school put on the play *Dracula* and asked me to help build the sets. When I showed up one night, I found several students in the middle of an argument.

"What's going on?" I asked.

"We're supposed to build a pair of French windows," a young woman named Maddie said. "But there's supposed to be a *door* here!"

"Ah," I said, understanding the problem. I looked at each of the students. "Do any of you know what French windows look like?"

They shook their heads.

I grabbed a pencil and quickly sketched a pair of French windows.

"They look like doors," a boy named Connor said.

"Bingo."

"They're *doors*?" Maddie asked.

"Yeah . . . they're *called* windows, but they're doors."

"We've got those at home!" Connor said, nodding emphatically. "Okay, I get it. I know what to do."

And with that, the crew built a perfect pair of French windows. Everything turned out well, but the kids had wasted a lot of time just because the director hadn't made certain they knew exactly what he wanted of them.

Here's another story, perhaps a bit silly. One day I asked a math class to do problems one through twenty-four on a certain page in their textbooks. The next day, a boy handed me a sheaf of papers half an inch thick.

"I hope you don't give us that much work every night," he grumbled.

"Twenty-four problems?" I asked. "What's the big deal?"

He blinked and then pounded himself on the head.

"Twenty-four problems? I thought you said *pages* one to twenty-four!"

Oops! We both learned a lesson that day!

Keep Your Communication Lines Open

Once you've told everyone what to do, you might think your work's done. But questions are certain to come up. There might be unexpected problems, and you need to be available to help out.

As a math teacher, whenever I'm teaching new concepts, I like to work out several problems with the class. After that, I'll put a problem on the board, give everyone time to try it, and then work it out so they can compare their work with mine. After several minutes of this, everyone ought to be able to do it, right?

Waaaaaay wrong!

It's usually not until everyone is working on their assignment that questions begin popping up. It's not until they're really on their own that some students realize they don't understand as well as they thought they did. And if I simply dove behind my desk, leaving everyone to figure things out on their own, some kids would never learn.

So stay close. Keep in touch. Check frequently for questions and complications that are certain to come up.

Be Willing to Listen

There's a famous story about a first aid instructor. He'd just taught his class to recognize the signs and symptoms of a heart attack when *he* had a heart attack!

He felt a dull pain in his chest. He wasn't able to catch his breath. His skin became cool and clammy.

"You're having a heart attack," one of his students announced.

"No," the teacher replied, clutching his chest. "I'm *not* having a heart attack." (Denial is actually a classic sign.)

As the symptoms became worse, the students finally took charge and called 911. And guess what? He really *was* having a heart attack!

The point is that the teacher wasn't willing to listen to his class. And he would have died if they hadn't taken charge and called for help.

You never know when someone in your group will come up with a great idea. So be willing to listen. More important, be a leader everyone will feel good about approaching with ideas, suggestions, or questions.

EFFECTIVE COMMUNICATION

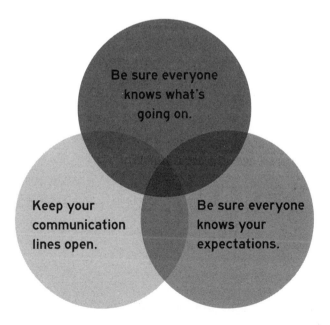

Be sure everyone knows what's going on.

Keep your communication lines open.

Be sure everyone knows your expectations.

To be an effective leader, the ability to communicate isn't optional. It's *critical*. So take the time to be sure everyone knows what's going on. Be certain they understand what you need from them. Keep in touch and be on the lookout for questions or problems. And finally, be willing to listen. Prove through your actions that you're approachable.

As you do these things, the quality of your work will improve by leaps and bounds. And you'll increase the chances of every project being a raging success!

ACTION STEPS!

- Think of a time you've been the victim of a mix-up in communication. What happened? _____

  _____

  _____

  _____

- What could you (or your leader) have done better?

  _____

  _____

  _____

- Think of a time you felt like "no one ever tells me anything." What happened? _____

  _____

  _____

  _____

- How could things have been better? _____

  _____

  _____

- Think of a time you had questions about a project or

assignment but had no one to ask. How did that make you feel? _____

_____

_____

- When I want my math students to make a poster (or some other project), I show them examples of good work other students have done. This not only shows everyone *exactly* what I'm looking for, but it also gets the creative juices flowing and inspires some students to come up with even better ideas. What can *you* do to show your group exactly what you want from them?

_____

_____

_____

- Think of the last time you gave instructions for something. On a scale of 1 to 10, with 1 being poor and 10 being very well, how effectively did you communicate your expectations? (Circle a number.)

  1   2   3   4   5   6   7   8   9   10

- What could you have done better? _____

_____

_____

- On a scale of 1 to 10, how available were you afterward to monitor progress or answer questions?

  1   2   3   4   5   6   7   8   9   10

- Is there anything you could have done better? If so, what? _____

_____

- How well did your group follow your directions?

(Did they do what you wanted? Did they meet your expectations?) _____

_____

_____

• What's one thing you can do better the next time you give instructions for a project or activity? _____

_____

_____

_____

Now, be sure to follow through. Be sure to give your ideas a try!

4 THE AMAZING TIME-TELLING DOG

MEETING THE NEEDS OF YOUR GROUP

I KNOW YOU WON'T BELIEVE THIS, but my dog can tell time.

Seriously!

Her name's Cinda, and she's a black lab I rescued from the animal shelter. She likes to chase balls, go for rides, and go walking at 3:30 in the morning. (I know it's early, but that's what we do!)

The amazing thing is that if I'm not up, she comes and gets me. I have no idea how she knows when it's time to go, but she doesn't let me sleep in. Ever.

One night I was out late and didn't get to bed until nearly midnight. I was sleeping soundly the next morning when I suddenly had a wet nose in my face.

"Oh, *yuck*!" I groaned, reaching out to push her away. "Doggy breath! I don't need that!"

I rolled over, hoping she'd take the hint and let me sleep in a bit. But she just thought I was playing a game. She jumped onto the bed and really put that wet nose to work. I glanced at the clock: 3:34.

Man, I thought. *How does she do that?*

But I crawled out of bed and got dressed. And a few minutes later we were out patrolling the neighborhood.

What really surprised me, though, was that we came across one of my neighbors watering her flowers.

"What in the world are *you* doing up so early?" I asked.

"Early? This is *late*!"

"You mean you haven't been to bed yet?"

"No," she said. "Night's still young."

I was amazed that anyone could possibly be up so late. On the other hand, she was astonished that anyone could be up so early.

But then, that's the way people are. We're all different. Sometimes *very* different. And to be an effective leader, you have to take everyone's differences into account.

Let me give you an example. At the school where I teach, we often give students doughnuts for earning good grades or having good attendance. Sounds good, huh?

Everyone thought so. But the first time they brought doughnuts into my classroom, I was amazed at how many students didn't want one!

You see, not everyone *likes* doughnuts. So our program is terrific for those students who do (and for those who get the extra doughnuts), but it's not so great for those who don't. Every term some students aren't recognized—or rewarded—because no one takes their tastes into account.

How would that make *you* feel?

As a leader, you have to understand that the members of your group are all unique. They all have different needs, different talents, and different interests. Some of them might like music. Others prefer sports. Some of them might love curling up with a good book, while others hate to read. And for you to be effective, you have to take those unique needs and characteristics into account.

I used to coach basketball. And I had drills and plays the whole team could run together. But when it came time to get serious, I'd separate my players according to their specific roles on the team. While my tall players practiced moving aggressively in the paint, I'd have the quick, short guys working on handling the ball, making pinpoint passes, and shooting from the outside.

It wouldn't have been productive to have my forwards and centers practice shooting three-pointers. And it would have been silly (not to mention a waste of time) to have my guards practicing posting up in the paint.

Instead, I coached the boys according to their individual strengths, abilities, and roles on the team.

You need to do the same thing with the members of your group. You need to identify their individual needs. You need to identify the traits that make them unique. And you need to find ways to meet those needs so each person contributes to the best of his or her ability.

This past school year, I had a boy named Ethan in my class. He was a great kid, full of energy and enthusiasm. But there were times he had a little *too* much energy. There were days he'd spend the entire period bouncing off the walls.

One day the principal brought a visitor in to watch my lesson. Do you think that calmed Ethan down any? Think again!

Every time I put a problem on the board, Ethan instantly had his hand in the air, waving frantically, excited to share the answer.

"Hold on," I told him once. "Give everyone a chance to figure it out."

"Can I come up and whisper it in your ear?"

"Yeah, sure."

And up he came, a huge grin across his face, to whisper the answer to me.

Ethan wasn't a bad kid, but his energy sometimes became distracting, not just to me, but to the other kids too. And for a while I wasn't certain what to do about it.

But one day it hit me. I couldn't just order him to sit quietly in his seat. With the amount of energy he was holding in, that would have been like asking a hurricane not to be windy.

So rather than try to bottle up his energy, I found ways to use it. I gave him errands, projects, and activities. I channeled his energy in positive, productive directions.

And not only did Ethan become one of my favorite students, but his grade improved too. After working off a little energy, he was able to settle down and put more effort into his assignments.

There wasn't anything magical about what I did. I simply recognized that one of my students had special needs, and then I found ways to meet them. And you can do the same thing in your group. One way to start is to make a chart like the one on the next

SHANE BARKER

page. List everyone's name, and beside it write one positive word that describes that person. You might use the word "athlete," for instance, to describe someone who's into sports. Or "musician" for someone who especially enjoys music. Keep these words positive, and try not to use the same word for more than one person.

Next, list the sort of things each person needs in his or her life—things that make him or her feel important or special. You might list such things as friends, attention, wearing nice clothes, being in charge, being noticed, and being the center of attention. Again, try to keep your observations positive.

Finally, list the traits that make each person unique. You might write things such as "outgoing," "energetic," "funny," "likes Star Wars," "enjoys school," or "likes listening to music."

When you're finished, your chart might look something like this (Notice that there is extra space at the bottom of each box. You'll see why in a moment.):

NAME/ DESCRIPTION	NEEDS	TRAITS
Dakota/Athlete	To be active, to have things to keep busy, to be given chances to work off energy	Is dependable; likes sports; has good leadership skills; has a good sense of humor; prefers outdoor activities
Ellen/Artist	To be noticed, to be given compliments, to have chances to perform	Is a great student; has straight As; likes to dress up; likes to read; enjoys music, concerts, plays, museums
Lexi/Model	To be given attention, to feel special, to have chances to stand out	Loves fashion, texting, shopping, BOYS, being with friends

Once you have your chart filled out, you have two goals: first, to find ways to meet each person's needs, and second, to find ways to use everyone's strengths to build the group.

Start by thinking of ways to meet each person's individual needs. If you have someone who loves being the center of attention, for instance, give him or her chances to show off!

Do you have someone who's bursting with energy? Give him something to do! Someone who craves attention? Give her a chance to stand out! Someone who feels insecure? Find ways to build his confidence!

Meeting the needs of your group will be one of the most important things you will ever do as a leader. And rest assured that your efforts will not go unnoticed. Or unrewarded.

Once you've begun meeting needs, start thinking of everyone's strengths. Everyone has them. And your job is not only to find them, but also to find ways to *use* them.

Do you have someone who's dynamic? Put her in charge of something! Someone who's creative? Ask him to help plan your next activity! Someone who's artistic? Get her to make a poster or banner! The possibilities are endless. So as you sit down to plan your next meeting, activity, or project, remember that you're not alone. Take a good look at the strengths of your group and put them to work!

As you consider each person's needs and traits, the following chart will help illustrate how it all fits together:

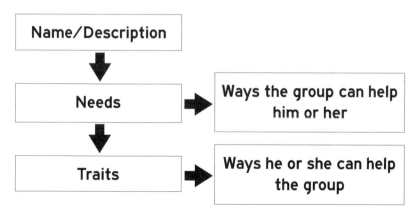

It's a simple chart, but let me show you how it might work with my friend Jason, who used to work for me at a Boy Scout camp.

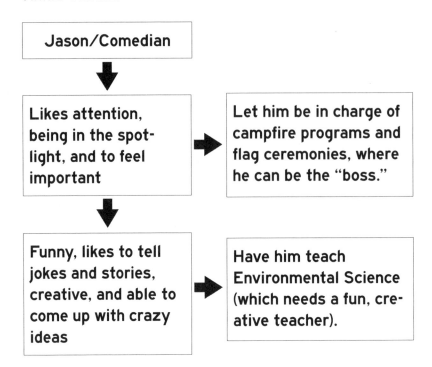

Ready to try it yourself? Think of someone in your group (preferably someone who could use a little attention). Now, considering that person's needs and traits, fill in the chart below:

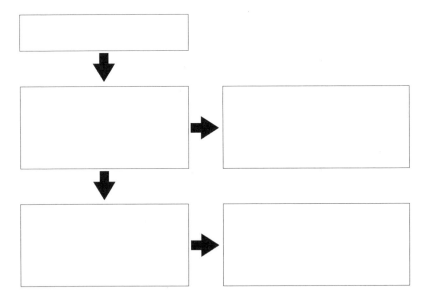

Finished?

How did it go?

If you're like me, it probably took a few minutes of careful thinking, but you should now have several good, concrete ideas for boosting and supporting that person *and* for using his or her strengths to improve the group too.

Now make a similar chart for each person in the group. Invite your advisors and counselors to help if you'd like, but find ways to build and support each person in the group and then find ways for each person to contribute. But don't stop there. Take action! Take the ideas you've written and get started on them.

I have a young friend named Keena who was in charge of the tech crew at her high school. That meant she was in charge of the lights, sound, and other electronics whenever there was an activity in the auditorium. There was a young man named Logan on her crew.

"Logan was a good techie," Keena said. "He was kind of shy and quiet, but he was good with electronics, and he liked working behind the scenes."

One day, though, she noticed several crew members standing around him. They were watching a video on his iPod.

"What's this?" she asked.

"Just a little movie I made."

Keena watched for a moment, amazed at how professional Logan's homemade movie seemed. "You *made* this?"

"Uh-huh."

Keena suddenly had an idea. She asked Logan to film the production they were working on. It turned out that Logan wasn't just a good cameraman, he was a talented editor too.

"He made the most amazing video," she said. "He did things with his camera that I never would have dreamed of."

But the most amazing thing was the difference it made to Logan.

"I couldn't believe how much he changed," Keena said. "He was always a nice kid, but he was shy. But once he started filming for us, he came right out of his shell."

What was the difference? A leader who found a way to make use of his talents and abilities.

Just imagine the difference you might make. Imagine the miracles you can be part of. So don't wait! Make your charts and work on them. Find ways to meet the needs of your group. Find ways to make use of your group members' strengths and talents.

Trust me, you'll do more than make a difference; you'll change lives! You'll work miracles! And you'll have a total blast as you do.

ACTION STEPS!

- Make a chart like the one illustrated in this chapter.

- List each person's name, along with a positive, one-word description of him or her.

- Fill in each person's needs as you see them. (Feel free to consult with your assistants or advisors if you need to.)

- Now, think of two things you can do to build, encourage, or support each person. List those things at the bottom of each box.

- Don't let your ideas sit idle. Choose one person from your group (preferably someone who could use a boost) and write his or her name here:

  _____

- Think of something you can do *today* to meet one of that person's needs, make him or her feel special, or boost his or her spirit. What is it? _____

  _____

  _____

  Now be sure to follow through and do it!

- Fill in each person's "trait" box. List things that set each person apart and make him or her special.

- Now, think of two things each person can do to help

the group. Write those things at the bottom of the trait box.

- Don't let your ideas gather dust! Choose one person randomly from your list and write his or her name here: _____

- Now think of something you could ask that individual to do *today* that would benefit the group. What is it?

  _____

  _____

  _____

  Ask today!

- Keep your chart where it's handy. Review it often and follow through with your action ideas.

5 HEY! SOMEONE'S PAINTED MY BATTING HELMET!

MAKING THE MOST OF YOUR RESOURCES

"YOU WANT ME to do *what?*"

"I want you to paint me a picture of a mountain man. Do you think you can do it?"

Sixteen-year-old Ryan Gifford pulled a face. I was the program director of a Cub Scout day camp, and Ryan was one of my assistants. Our camp was called "Jeremiah Johnson" after a nineteenth-century trapper; I thought that a painting of a mountain man on the camp gate would be a classy touch.

Ryan scratched his head as I explained it to him. "Why are you asking *me?*"

"Because you like to draw."

Ryan laughed. "Yeah, I like to draw. But that doesn't mean I'm good at it!"

He thought for a moment. "You know who you should ask?"

"Who?"

"Natalie."

"Natalie?" I blinked, picturing a popular young woman who was one of the real "movers and shakers" of my young staff. She had the personality of a bottle rocket, the voice of Hannah Montana, and the determination of the Energizer Bunny. But I had no idea she was artistic too. "Can she paint?"

Ryan laughed again. "Have you ever been to the high school?"

"Sure."

41

"Been in the office?"

"A time or two."

"Did you happen to see a painting of a bear?"

"The bear standing in the river? Yeah, it's really—wait . . . are you telling me *Natalie* painted that?"

"Yeah. She also won a bunch of money in a contest once, and I think she's even got a scholarship to some big art school."

I had no idea. And I felt pretty silly scrounging for artists when I had a fantastic artist already working for me.

There's an important lesson in that story. You see, you're likely to have artists in your group too. You're likely to have writers, photographers, singers, actors, comedians, mathematicians, machinists, wood carvers, scholars, and athletes. And your ability to identify and then make use of those resources will set you apart as a leader.

A Boy Scout troop I know once spent three hundred dollars renting canoes for a river trip, only to find out the father of one of the boys already owned everything they needed.

"Why didn't you tell me that your dad owned canoes?" the Scoutmaster asked.

The Scout just shrugged. "You never asked me."

You need to remember that most people like being able to help. They enjoy being able to contribute. They appreciate opportunities to show off their skills and talents. Not only that, but by making the most of people's skills and talents, the work you do will turn out better too.

I'm embarrassed to admit this, but I was at school one day trying to format something on my computer, and I kept messing it up. We have a full-time computer specialist in the building who could have helped, but he's always busy.

And then it hit me. I had thirty-eight teenagers in the room. And who knows computers better than teenagers?

I tried to act casual. "Do any of you, um, know anything about computers?"

Hands shot up all over the room. And the next instant I was surrounded by aspiring hackers just itching to get their hands on my computer. And I learned more about formatting in the next five minutes than I had in the last five years.

School computer specialist? Who needed him?

Another time I was trying to make a poster for the wall. I had rulers, markers, and stencils, but it was taking forever, and it wasn't looking all that good either.

And then it hit me again. (Okay . . . sometimes I can be a little slow.)

I looked up and asked, "Are any of you good at lettering?"

A hand rose from the side of the room.

"Oh, Maili! I should have remembered! Would you mind helping me for a minute?"

And then—in mere minutes—Maili made a poster that was absolutely fantastic.

What a lesson! I could have spent hours working on that poster myself, and it never would have looked half as good as the one Maili made in just a few minutes. *That's* why you use your resources!

Remember that there's no sense wasting time trying to hand-stitch a costume if you have a seamstress who can do the job in ten minutes. There's no sense renting camping equipment if someone has everything you need gathering dust in the garage.

The question is, how do you know what resources are available to you? How do you know what skills and abilities you have that you can make use of?

The best idea is to start with a survey. Make a chart like the one on the following page, modifying it to fit the needs of your group. Then make copies and pass them out. Tell everyone to fill them out and not to be shy about it!

Okay, got them all?

Good! Now hang onto them. Put them in a notebook or binder where you can keep track of them. Some of your group's skills and abilities might seem unimportant now, but you never know what might suddenly come in handy next week or next month.

Also, be sure to use the "notes" section at the bottom of the chart to list things you later learn about each person. And don't forget to get surveys from new members who join the group later.

PERSONAL RESOURCE SURVEY

Check the box that best applies to you	Very Skilled	Somewhat Skilled	Not Skilled	Not Skilled but Would Like to Learn
Painting				
Writing				
Drawing				
Singing				
Musical Instruments (Which)				
Leading Music				
Sports				
Acting				
Drama				
Debate				
Building Things				
Scrapbooking				
Photography				

Other hobbies and interests _____

Best school subjects _____

Tools, equipment, and supplies (camping equipment, boats, trucks, athletic supplies, and so forth) you have access to (and would be willing to share) _____

_____

Other notes:

All finished? Good!

Now that you know your resources, use them! But don't just look for people who can help out with your next project or activity: look for ways to put everyone else to work too.

Is someone in the group good with numbers? Put him in charge of your budget! Is there someone who likes making scrapbooks? Ask her to be the group historian! Someone who likes to write? Maybe he could write an article for the school paper or maybe even a local newspaper. Someone who likes to sing or to lead music? Put her in charge of opening ceremonies, if you have them, or put her in charge of morale. Try to find some job or position that each person can take charge of, giving him or her a chance to make a unique mark on the group.

I once had an artist on my baseball team. (Okay, there's a challenge: finding a way to make use of an artist on a baseball team!) We were called the Bats, and I had an idea. I collected all of our batting helmets and then yelled for Cooper.

"You wanna do something really cool?" I asked.

"Sure."

"Then how about taking our helmets home and painting them for us?"

"Our batting helmets?"

"Sure! You could paint 'em so they're all nice and shiny . . . and then you could paint bats on them."

Cooper grinned. "*Bats?* Seriously?"

"Seriously. Are you interested?"

"You bet!"

And he was. He painted the helmets a dark, glossy blue and then painted Batman's bat symbol on the sides of each one. They were the coolest batting helmets in the league.

There was another boy on the team who enjoyed rebuilding cars with his dad. (They'd start with an old, rusted piece of junk in the driveway. A couple of months later they'd have a nice, shiny car parked out front with a For Sale sign in the window.)

"How would you like to do me a favor?" I asked him one day.

"Sure. What do you need?"

I handed him an old, aluminum bat. "Think you could fill that with dirt?"

"What?"

"To warm up with," I explained. "Having a nice, heavy bat to swing would help loosen guys up before they hit. Think you could drill a hole in the handle so we could fill it with dirt, and then plug it back up with a bolt or something?"

"Piece of cake."

Well, I managed to make use of an artist and a machinist . . . on my baseball team!

Now, what about you? Can you think of a way to use a musician in your group? A woodworker? An actor? A wrestler? Just for fun, try to think of a way you could use a rodeo rider in your group.

A rodeo rider?

Hey, they're out there! And they're usually pretty passionate about riding, roping, and whooping it up! So if you can find a way to harness that excitement and put it to work, who knows what you might accomplish!

The next time you're planning an activity, a project, a party, or an outing, see how creative you can be with your resources. Try using people you might not normally think of (giving everyone a chance to pitch in). Try using people in ways you haven't done before, stretching your creativity.

You might be surprised by how well things turn out. And you might discover resources you didn't know you had.

Not only that, but you'll build confidence, enthusiasm, and loyalty in your group that will result in phenomenal results and send you blasting toward success.

Don't wait. Start now!

ACTION STEPS!

- Make a chart like the one listed in this chapter for each member of your group. (Don't know how to use a computer? Use your resources! Ask around and find someone who does!) Have everyone fill it out at your next meeting.

- Think of some job, assignment, project, or chore you have coming up. Write it down here: _____

  _____

- Now look through your surveys and find someone whose skills would be perfect for helping out. Who is it? _____

  _____

  Don't put it off. Ask that person to help out *today*!

- Close your eyes and pick a survey at random from the stack. Whose is it? _____

- Now, take a good look at his or her skills and talents and come up with a creative or unusual way that person could contribute to the group. Describe it here:

  _____

  _____

  _____

  Ask him or her *today*!

- Choose a member of your group who doesn't normally get a lot of attention. Who is it? _____

- Now think of some way for him or her to contribute. Look for a way that individual can show off his or her skills and talents. Describe your idea here: _____

  _____

  _____

  Ask him or her today!

- Keep your surveys handy. Complete these action steps again in a month—or a week!

6 THE SPEAKER'S GONNA BE LATE!

PLANNING FOR SUCCESS

"UH-OH."

Carly Van Cott looked up from the plates of cookies and brownies she was arranging.

"What?" she asked, not liking the sound of her friend Kamryn's voice. "What are you uh-ohing about?"

Kamryn Price gestured across the cultural hall. "Sister Murdock just walked in, and she doesn't look very happy."

Carly looked. Sure enough, the stake Young Women president had the expression of a little kid who'd heard that Christmas had just been cancelled.

The Young Women were preparing for girls' camp, and Carly was the stake youth representative. They had organized a special fireside to help everyone spiritually prepare for a fantastic week in the mountains, and young women from all over the stake were already filling the chapel.

Carly had helped to plan the evening. She'd made arrangements for the building and the refreshments, and with Sister Murdock's approval, she'd invited a popular youth speaker to talk. She felt a twinge of nervousness at the look on Sister Murdock's face.

"What's wrong?"

"Sister Frost just called," the president said. Sister Frost was the speaker Carly had invited. "There's some kind of emergency, and she's not going to be able to make it tonight."

"Oh, that's too bad!" Carly said. "I was really looking forward to hearing her!"

She glanced toward the chapel, noting how full it was getting, and then brightened.

"Well, that just means we'll have to go to Plan B."

"Plan B?" Kamryn asked. "We have a Plan B?"

Carly nodded. "Rachel Young's mother is an expert camper. She even wrote a book about it. I asked her if she'd mind speaking if there were any problems."

"When did you do that?"

"A couple of weeks ago," Carly said nonchalantly. She looked at Sister Murdock. "Hey, you're the one who always says, 'Hope for the best, but plan for the worst!'"

I was impressed with Carly's foresight. There are few things as important to good leadership as an ability to plan. And if you've ever taken part in a poorly planned activity, you already know that. There's nothing worse than sitting around, wasting time, while someone figures out what everyone's supposed to be doing.

Several years ago I helped build the sets for a school play. Our director was a genius of planning and organization. Every night he knew exactly which scenes to rehearse, which actors and actresses he'd need, and when he'd need them. Cast members who weren't needed were assigned classrooms where they could rehearse on their own. Meanwhile, the set and stage crews were told exactly what they needed to work on, with deadlines for getting it all done.

The nice thing was that no one ever felt that his or her time was being wasted. No one was ever left sitting around, wondering what to do next. The director kept everyone busy, and every night we went home knowing that we'd made progress and that we were that much closer to being ready for opening night.

Being an effective leader requires the ability to plan just like that. So what should you plan for?

Everything!

Plan your meetings, projects, activities, rehearsals, practices, parties, and performances. Everything! Make certain you know exactly what you need to get done, what help you're going to need, who's going to do what, and what materials you'll need.

And be sure to write it all down! There's nothing worse than having a crystal-clear image of an activity in your mind only to forget some key element.

You might consider using a worksheet like the one on the next page, modifying it to meet the needs of your group and the specific activity you're planning.

Like many things, an ability to plan is not something everyone is automatically born with. So as you're gaining experience, here are a few ideas to help you along.

Be Sure that You Have More than Enough to Do

Several years ago, my junior high school changed from a traditional schedule with forty-five-minute classes to an A-B schedule with eighty-minute classes.

Whew! That's a long time to spend in a math class!

As we were preparing to make the change, we were warned again and again to plan at least two more activities than we thought we'd have time for each period. And *that* was great advice!

I can't tell you how many times I outlined a lesson, certain it would take every possible minute, only to finish and still have twenty minutes left!

When you plan activities, keep that in mind. Make certain that you have more than enough games, projects, or activities. If you never get to some activities, fine. That's a lot better than doing everything you have planned and still having thirty or forty minutes left! (If you're conducting an hour-long *meeting* and finish early, though, send everyone home! Don't keep everyone sitting around if you've finished your business and have nothing more to discuss!)

As a ski patrolman, I'm required to carry a medical pack whenever I'm on duty. As I pack my supplies, I often wonder how many splints and bandages I should carry. I always toss in more than I need, but I know it's better to have a few too many than even one too few.

And that's the rule I use whenever I make plans too.

Planning Worksheet

Activity:

Date:

Time:

Purpose:
Exactly what do you need to accomplish?

Location:
Do you need to make any arrangements for this? If so, who is the best person to make them?

Material, equipment, or supplies needed:
Can you obtain any of this from members of the group? Which members? If not, is someone in the group able to obtain them?

Warm-up Activities (if appropriate):
Is there someone you could delegate to take care of this?:

Main Activity:
Describe what you're going to do, how you're going to do it, who's going to do what, and how long you expect it to take.

Wrap-up Activities (if appropriate):

PLAN B:
What will you do if something goes wrong, if supplies run out, the weather turns bad, or anything else threatens to ruin everything?

Be Flexible

I used to coach a lot, and I was always fanatical about planning, even if it was just for a simple basketball practice. (My players all knew that and often teased me about it. We were scrimmaging one night, when every light in the building suddenly went out. As we stood in the darkness—unable to see our hands in front of our faces—the team clown said, "This is all part of the plan, right, Coach?")

Anyway, I always planned on having ten players. But there were nights when not everyone came. And I had to be flexible enough to make things work anyway.

Be aware that the same thing will happen to you. When it does, remember that your plans are just *guidelines*. They're just *tools*. They're not laws you have to stick to in order to ensure the survival of the universe.

So if something comes up—if you have more or fewer people than you planned for, if the gym or rec hall suddenly becomes unavailable, or if something else happens to disrupt things—be flexible enough to adapt. Be willing to change your plans to fit the situation.

I'm sorry to mention sports again, but I once showed up to baseball practice with an organized, detailed, well-thought-out plan in hand. We had a big game coming up, and there were a few wrinkles I thought we needed to work out in order to win.

As the boys were warming up, one of my team captains walked up.

"Hey, Coach . . . how 'bout letting us play workups today?"

I just laughed. Workups were a game we sometimes played for a change of pace. It didn't improve anyone's skills a whole lot, but it involved a lot of action and was always fun.

"After we beat the Dodgers we can play workups," I said. "But right now we've got a lot of work to do."

Bryan gave me the same look my dog does when I'm pretending that I don't have another treat in my pocket.

"We've been working pretty hard, Coach," he reminded me. "Maybe we *need* to have a little fun for a change."

I looked at him for a moment. I valued his opinion, and I

knew he didn't make suggestions he didn't feel strongly about.

"Tell you what," I said. "You guys give me a good half hour of solid infield/outfield, and we'll spend the rest of the time playing workups."

"Buy us doughnuts?"

"Don't push it."

"How 'bout if we beat the Dodgers?"

"You beat the Dodgers, and I'll buy you pizza."

"All right!"

He dashed off to share the good news, and the instant I heard the cheers I knew I'd made the right decision.

Remember that you're the boss, not your plans. Don't feel like you have to accomplish everything you've planned just because it's written down. Be willing to make changes and adjustments to meet changing situations and circumstances.

Plan for Emergencies

When I was in charge of Cub Scout camp, I developed a schedule that we adjusted and refined over the summer until it seemed perfect.

But because it was an outdoor camp, I always had a Plan B ready. There was always a chance of unexpected rain or thunderstorms, so I kept a list of games and activities on hand in case the weather ever forced us under the camp pavilions.

It turns out I never needed them. But having them planned and ready was far better than watching a storm come boiling over the mountains and not having anything prepared.

When I first became a teacher, I heard someone say, "Never waste your students' time." And that's great advice for any leader. And the first, best way to do that is to plan well. Make that one of your habits today!

ACTION STEPS!

- Make a planning worksheet like the one illustrated in this chapter. (Feel free to modify it for your particular needs.) Then use it to plan your next project or activity.

- Write down two things people can do while they're waiting for your next activity to start: _____

  _____

- Think about a meeting, practice, or activity you have coming up. Now look through your resource surveys and identify two people who are especially qualified to help out. Write their names here: _____

  _____

- Ask them *today* if they have suggestions or ideas for making the activity more successful.

- Think of someone in the group who needs a little extra attention. Write his or her name here: _____

- Think of some way you can use that person in your next activity, giving him or her a chance to contribute or feel special. Write your idea here: _____

  _____

  _____

  _____

  Don't wait! Ask him or her today!

- Write down three things you can do if you end up having extra time at your next activity: _____

  _____

  _____

- Suppose someone's not participating during your next activity. Write down three ideas for encouraging him or her to join in: _____

  _____

  _____

- What's your backup plan in case something goes wrong? Write it here: _____

  _____

  _____

- It's better to be safe than sorry. Write down one more thing you can do if something goes wrong or falls through: _____

  _____

  _____

- Is there someone in the group who doesn't always show up? If so, think of some way to "entice" him or her to come out. Is there something you can do to spark that person's interest? Something you can ask that person to do to get him or her more involved? Someone in the group who could extend a special invitation or even pick that person up to make sure he or she comes? Write your idea here: _____

  _____

  _____

  _____

  Be sure to follow through!

- Remember to be flexible. Be willing to adapt to changing situations. Remind yourself that *you're* the boss, not your plan.

7

HOW TO EARN A PIZZA

ENERGIZING YOUR GROUP WITH GOALS

"PIZZA! Pizza! Pizza!"

The seventh-grade football players were hopping in unison as they chanted.

"Pizza! Pizza! Pizza!"

Coach Williams shook his head. "Sorry, guys. Not tonight."

The energized football players weren't taking no for an answer. They jumped faster, chanting even louder. "Pizza! Pizza! *Pizza!*"

Coach Williams held up a hand, trying to mask a smile. "Sorry, guys . . . can't afford it. Coach Barker and I nearly went broke feeding you all the last time."

The coach's response just got the boys even more excited. "*Pizza! Pizza! Pizza!*"

The coach's shoulders dropped as he turned to look at me. I shrugged, putting a hand up to my face to keep from smiling.

"All right," the coach finally said, pretending to surrender.

The boys exploded with cheers.

The coach glanced at me and grinned: he had the boys right where he wanted them.

The week before, Coach Williams had given the team what he called the "Hundred-Yard Challenge."

"Give me a hundred yards total offense tonight," he said before the game, "and Coach Barker and I will buy pizza for everyone."

The kids were instantly excited even though the coach had a couple of conditions.

"If you *lose* yards," he warned, "if you let your quarterback get sacked, those yards get subtracted from your total."

An offensive lineman named Derrick blew a raspberry. "Oh, like we're gonna let *that* happen."

The coach just grinned. "And every yard the other team gains gets subtracted, too."

"What if we sack *their* quarterback?" a cocky linebacker asked.

"Every yard they lose gets added to your total."

"All *right*!"

I couldn't believe what a difference the coach's challenge made. The kids tore into the game with the energy of wild horses. Offensive tackles exploded off the line, plowing into blitzing linebackers and knocking them silly. Receivers leaped and stretched like Olympic gymnasts as they pulled down passes. Running backs pounded the field like stampeding bulls, bulldozing defensive safeties and scrambling for every last inch they could get. It was incredible to watch!

The kids got their hundred yards, all right. And just happened to win the game too. Now they wanted to do it again.

That's the magic of goals. Exciting, creative goals will work miracles in your group too, especially if the group ever slips into a rut or needs a shot of momentum. Goals can energize, motivate, and inspire everyone to keep on track and get the job done.

I have a young friend named Kayla who was in a high school play. A week or two before opening night, the director had a meeting with the cast and crew.

"There are seven hundred seats in this auditorium," he said, gesturing toward the sea of empty chairs. "I'd like to see every one of them filled opening night."

He let everyone glance around the auditorium for a moment before continuing.

"I know it looks like a lot of seats. I know it seems like a big challenge. But I know you can do it. I think you owe it to yourselves to do it. After all the time and work you've put into this production, you owe it to yourselves to pack this place every single night!"

The director's enthusiasm was so contagious that everyone caught it. The cast and crew began canvassing the school and the community, passing out fliers and invitations and asking everyone they knew to come. Innovative cast members got local newspapers to write stories and even convinced a TV station to run a short promo feature.

Did it make a difference?

"We sold out every night!" Kayla told me. "We had to turn so many people away that we ended up running the show for an extra week!"

As you look for ways to motivate and inspire your group, goals can be one of your most powerful tools. And they can do more than spur your group into action. They can light fires beneath struggling, uninspired individuals, sparking them to work harder, stretch farther, and run faster. Sounds good, doesn't it?

I have a book of stamps I use for paying bills and mailing letters. It was getting low on stamps, though, and I knew I soon had to make a trip to the post office.

I happened to be writing a certain book at the time, and I decided that I wouldn't allow myself to buy stamps until I went to the post office to mail off my book.

Suddenly I had a goal. I had to finish my book before I ran out of stamps. And every time I needed a stamp to pay a bill or mail a letter, I had an instant, visual reminder to get back to work.

Did it work? I made it with two stamps to spare.

I hope you've got the vision by now. Exciting goals can charge everyone's batteries and boost their adrenalin levels. But to make your goals as effective as possible, you need to follow a few guidelines.

First, set goals that are *specific*. Deciding to become a better quorum, a better team, or a better band might sound like a good goal. But how do you measure something like that? And how do you know when you've accomplished it?

Better, more specific goals would be to achieve 100 percent attendance at a merit badge powwow, score forty points in the next game, or qualify for the regional festival. Specific goals might include everyone making the school honor roll, earning two merit badges, running two miles a day, or having their parts memorized by the end of the week.

Goals like that are specific. And measurable. People working toward specific goals know exactly what they need to do and exactly how close they are to reaching them. And they'll know exactly when they've achieved them.

Second, be sure that your goals are *reasonable*. Winning the state championship might sound like an awesome goal. But if you're a team of freshmen—and you're playing against seniors who've been teammates since the third grade—you might not have much of a chance.

At first, high, lofty goals might get everyone excited. But later, when they prove to be unreachable, they'll discourage everyone. And that's worse than having no goals at all.

It's better—and more effective—to choose goals that are difficult enough to stretch your muscles but not so hard it'll take a blast from Dumbledore's wand to achieve them.

Take a moment to evaluate your own goals with the following checklist:

Goals Checklist

	Yes	No
Is it specific? (Do you know exactly what you want to accomplish?)	____	____
Is it measurable? (Will you be able to tell when you're done?)	____	____
Is it reasonable? (Is it something you can actually pull off?)	____	____
Is it challenging? (Will you have to work or stretch to reach it?)	____	____

A third tip is to break your goals down into smaller, bite-sized chunks.

Think of your goal as a flight of stairs. If you want to climb to the top of a tall building, those hundreds (or thousands) of steps might seem intimidating. But if you focus on just getting to the top of the first floor, you suddenly have a more manageable goal, one you know you can reach. So you jump into action, taking the stairs two at a time, and make it to the top of the first floor.

Wow! You've just accomplished something, haven't you? How does that feel? Pretty good, right? After all, you've just completed a goal! And that fires you up, so you set your sights on the next floor, and off you go. And by taking the steps a floor at a time, you eventually get to the top.

Now, suppose you set some personal goal for yourself, like earning an A in Killer Biology. That might seem like a pretty lofty achievement. And you may not even think it's possible. But if you break it up into smaller, bite-sized tasks, it's suddenly not so frightening.

Think you could get an A on the first assignment?

Sure you can!

Get an A on your first quiz?

No problem!

Get an A on your first lab, project, or research paper?

No sweat! Just buckle down, put in the time, and get it done!

See how it works? The trick is breaking big goals into smaller chunks and then taking things one step at a time. That way, things are more manageable and less intimidating. After all, you ought to be able to get an A on *one* measly assignment, right? And *anyone* can get an A on one quiz, can't they?

Take a look at a goal you are working on and identify the intermediate steps you'll need to achieve on the way.

What's the first step you'll need to take?

The second step?

The third step?

You see? Any large goal can be broken down into more manageable steps. And if you attack your goal one step at a time, it'll be easier to manage. It'll be easier to keep track of and easier to accomplish.

I know a young man named Garrett who was competing at a Shakespearean festival. He had a particularly long monologue to memorize, and at first it seemed almost overwhelming.

"It was huge!" Garrett said. "And it was written in old English that's not so easy to understand anyway."

Garrett said the part was so difficult that he became discouraged and was even tempted to quit.

"But my director knew what I was going through," he said. "He told me to just concentrate on the first paragraph. It wasn't very long and didn't take me long to learn. And then I just learned the second paragraph, and then the third. And before I knew it, I had the whole thing down cold."

That was a good strategy!

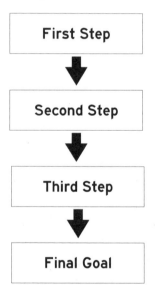

I have a friend named Jessica who plays competitive soccer. At the first of the season, her team only had one goal: to beat their biggest rivals, the Strikers.

But they worked and practiced and then worked some more . . . and beat the Strikers 4–3. And they suddenly realized that, "Hey! If we can beat them, we can beat anybody!"

So they set another goal: to win the region tournament. And then they went back to work, practicing and training as hard as they could, and came home with the region crown.

That really set them on fire! So now they set their sights as high as they could, taking aim at the state championship.

Do I really need to tell you how *that* turned out?

For Jessica's team, realistic, attainable goals were the motivation they needed to push themselves. Their goals gave everyone something to work for, to become excited about, and to stretch for. Their goals got everyone pumped up and energized.

When I was working at Scout Camp, I once walked into a campsite to see fifty playing cards pinned to the wall of the pavilion.

"What's this?" I asked.

"Party cards!" the Scouts shouted at once.

"*Party* cards? What're party cards?"

"Every time one of us finishes a merit badge we get to take a card down," one of the boys explained.

"Yeah! And if we get all fifty—"

"—our Scoutmaster's taking us to the water park!"

"Sweet!" I said.

It sounded like a good plan. And as the week went on, I kept track of the troop's party cards. A few of them came down the first day. (There are a couple of "easy" merit badges.) By Wednesday, they were about half gone. On Friday morning there were twelve cards still pinned to the wall.

And that's when the party cards really paid off.

"Every year we go home with a bunch of half-finished merit badges," the senior patrol leader told me. "But not this year. You just watch."

And he was right. Those Scouts—motivated by the promise of a party and the thrill of pulling cards off the wall—went to work. Boys who might have stopped short buckled down, pushed themselves, and went the extra mile to get every last requirement signed off.

I was passing the campsite later in the afternoon when I heard a huge cheer.

"What's going on?" I asked.

"Our last card!" someone shouted. "We just took down the last card!"

And a few weeks later that troop of adrenaline-charged Scouts was wreaking havoc at the water park and having a great time.

Challenging, stimulating goals can work miracles in your group too. So don't hesitate to use them. Let them motivate, energize, and inspire your group and send the whole bunch of you roaring toward success!

ACTION STEPS!

- Think of a goal that would energize your group. (You can come up with one yourself, or you can choose one as a group.) Write it here: _____

    _____

- What's something you can do *today* to get everyone started on it? _____

    _____

    _____

    (Now get up and get going!)

- Break your goal into smaller, bite-sized chunks. List at least five of those chunks here:

    1.
    2.
    3.
    4.
    5.

- Choose something from the list above you could get started on today. What is it? _____

    _____

    (Go do it!)

- Find some way to remind everyone what they're working toward. Remember party cards? A flashy sign or poster will help to remind everyone what you're working for. Write your idea here: _____

  _____

  _____

- Consider your resources. Which members of your group would best be able to help you reach your goal?

  _____

  _____

- How can they help? _____

  _____

  _____

  Ask them today!

8 ▶ I'VE BEEN HIT BY LIGHTNING . . . AGAIN!
EVALUATING YOUR PROGRESS

CRACK!

The clap of thunder boomed over the mountain, rumbling for several seconds like the growl of an angry tyrannosaurus. The next instant, the clouds opened up and poured rain like a waterfall.

"Wow!" my friend Jake said, peering into the darkness. "That was close!"

He winced as another flash of lightning split the night sky and then asked, "Is it true lightning never strikes the same place twice?"

"Yes!" a kid named Brandon replied.

"How do you know?"

" 'Cause after the first time, the place isn't there anymore!"

Everyone laughed. A boy named Alec said, "I heard about a guy who got struck by lightning seven times!"

"Seven times? No way!"

"That's what I heard."

"And he *lived*?"

"Guess so. . . . But I've always wondered: if a guy gets struck by lightning seven times and *lives* . . . is he lucky or unlucky?"

I laughed. "After the first two or three times I think *I'd* stop going outside when it's raining!"

Everyone laughed again, enjoying the nighttime fireworks. We'd been backpacking through the mountains of New Mexico for seven days. And it had rained for all but two of them.

The first night we'd gotten pretty wet. (My tent partner actually left the tent flaps open while we were out hiking, and we came back to find our sleeping bags floating in an inch of water.)

But over the next couple of days, we learned how to camp in the rain. We learned, for instance, to get our campsites up and ready before the storms hit each afternoon. We learned to pitch our tents on slopes that channeled the runoff away. We learned to put tarps *inside* our tents, rather than underneath.

By the end of the trip, we'd become so good at staying dry we were able to sit back and actually enjoy the storms.

How did we do that?

We learned from our mistakes. Every morning we took the time to figure out what we'd done right and what we'd done wrong. We learned a lot of lessons the hard way, but we never made the same mistake twice. We made a point of evaluating how we were doing and then made adjustments. And every night we got a little better . . . and we stayed a little drier.

And *that* is an important key to good leadership.

As a schoolteacher, I constantly evaluate what I'm doing. Every day my lessons change from class to class. Every period I keep track of what's working, what's not, and what problems my students have. The next period I make adjustments.

Sometimes an activity I'm really excited about will go over as well as soggy oatmeal, so I'll throw it out and try something else.

And sometimes things unexpectedly turn out better than expected, so I'll ramp them up and make them even better for the next class.

We learn by doing. And to be a good leader, you constantly need to evaluate how things are going for you. If a certain activity isn't working, try to figure out why. If the problem is something you can fix, make adjustments. But if it turns out the activity's just bad, toss it out and try something else.

Likewise, when you find an activity that gets everyone fired up and asking for more, figure out why it's so good. If you can figure out *why* a game or project is successful, you might be able to apply that secret to other activities too.

Take a minute to think about your group's most recent activity. It doesn't matter if you were in charge or not; just think about how it went.

Was it fun? Was it successful? Did it accomplish its purpose?

If you answered yes to any of those questions, try to figure out *why* it worked out so well. *Why* was it fun? *Why* was it successful? *How* did it build trust, teach a lesson, or accomplish whatever it was supposed to?

Now, what have you learned? Have you identified any strategies you can apply to your *next* activity?

And if you answered no to any of those original questions, try to pinpoint exactly what went wrong. Why *wasn't* it fun? Why *wasn't* it successful? Why *didn't* it accomplish anything?

As you answer these questions, keep track of things to avoid next time!

When I was in college learning to become a teacher, I had to spend time observing actual teachers at work. I remember watching one teacher who took nearly ten minutes to call roll.

Holy cow, I thought. *What a waste of time!* And I vowed that when I became a teacher myself, I'd find a better way to do that.

Later, I was sitting in a faculty meeting in which the speaker spent his entire presentation reading from note cards that weren't organized.

All right, I thought, *if I ever get a chance to do that, I'm going to dazzle everybody! I'm* not *going to bore everyone to death, and I'm not going to read my whole presentation!*

Over the years, I've learned a lot by watching other teachers, "borrowing" ideas I liked, learning from their mistakes, and mapping out plans for myself. And I've learned even more by evaluating how well those ideas worked for me.

Evaluating is one of the most critical principles of leadership because it's the step in which we *learn*. It's the step in which we *grow*. And it's the step in which we *progress*.

The next time you finish a lesson, an activity, or an outing, take the time to evaluate how it went. You can do this with your assistants and advisors or you might choose to do it by yourself.

Either way, don't pass up the opportunity to learn from the

experience. Keep track of things you'll definitely want to try again. And identify things that didn't work well but that you can improve on or skip the next time.

You can start by making a chart like this:

ACTIVITY:

Which things went really well? Why?	
Which things didn't go so well? Why?	
Which things would I do again? Why?	
Which things would I skip next time? Why?	
Which things could I do better? (And how could I *make* them better?)	
What new things could I try next time?	

As you fill in the blanks, analyzing how things went, you'll learn. But don't stop there! Be sure to take action and apply what you've learned to your next project.

I have a young friend named Nicci whose family has a tradition called QKS.

"It stands for Quit, Keep, and Start," she explained. "Every so often my parents will take one of us kids aside and say, 'QKS.' Then they'll tell us one thing they want us to *quit* doing, one thing they want us to *keep* doing, and one thing they want us to *start* doing."

And it works both ways. If there's something about the family—or one of the parents—that the children don't like, they're allowed to QKS too.

The system isn't as formal as the chart we just talked about. But it does allow everyone in the family to evaluate what's going on and to suggest improvements.

STEPPING UP, TAKING CHARGE & LEADING THE WAY

And that's something you can do too. Think about your group for a moment. If you had to choose, is there one thing you'd like everyone to *quit* doing? Anything you definitely want everyone to *keep* doing? And is there anything you'd really like them to *start* doing?

See? If you took the time to answer those three questions, you now have three ideas you can use to improve your group.

A couple of years ago, I signed up to take what the ski patrol calls the Senior Emergency Medical Management test. Each candidate skis up to simulated "accidents," where they find several victims. And then that person is judged on how well he or she responds to and manages the situation.

It's a challenging test, and I'd heard horror stories about how hard it is to pass. (My instructor, in fact, told us time and time again that he'd failed it *his* first time.)

At any rate, eight patrollers from my resort were scheduled to take the test, and for weeks we met every Saturday night to practice. Volunteers acted as victims while "judges" watched and took notes as we took turns responding to imaginary accidents.

It was tough! But after each scenario, we took time to talk about how we'd done. We talked about those things we'd done right, things we'd forgotten, things we'd messed up, and things we could do better.

It was hard for me to hear people point out my mistakes (it seems like I always got more "suggestions" than compliments). But what a difference it made!

Within a couple of weeks my medical skills had improved by leaps and bounds. When I responded to actual accidents on the mountain, I performed like some kind of medical superman. (Okay, I wasn't really a superman, but I was a thousand times better than I'd been before!)

Those informal evaluations taught me more than all the hours I'd spent sitting in classrooms put together. They improved my skills—and confidence—more than I ever believed possible.

And good, thoughtful evaluations can do the same for you.

Try this: think about the last test you took in school. Remember it?

All right, how well did you do?

Were you satisfied with your score?

Did you study as hard as you could have? (Or did you put things off until the last minute?)

Is there anything you could have done to earn a better score? (And even if you received a good score, is there anything you could have done better? What?)

Now, *what can you do to get an even better score next time?*
Finished?

Okay, now that was a simple exercise. But by answering those questions, did you come up with any ways to do better on your next test?

See? Now imagine how evaluating can help you to improve your group's next project or activity!

Remember that evaluating isn't just a good idea. It's critical if you want your group to be successful. It's an essential step for improving everything you do.

So don't put it off! Make it part of everything you do!

ACTION STEPS!

- Think of a recent lesson, project, or activity you've been part of. (If possible, think of one you've actually been in charge of.) What was it? _____

  _____

- Describe one thing that went really well:

  _____

  _____

  _____

- Can you identify why it was successful? Is there some way you can apply that to future activities? How? _____

  _____

  _____

- What's one thing you could have done better?

  _____

  _____

- What exactly could you have done to make things more exciting, more interesting, or more entertaining?

  _____

  _____

  _____

- Is there some part of the activity you'd leave out next time? Why? _____

  _____

  _____

- On a scale of 1 to 10, how prepared were you for the activity? Circle a number:

  1   2   3   4   5   6   7   8   9   10

- What number *should* you have circled? (And do you need to prepare better next time?) List three things you could do to better prepare yourself next time: _____

  _____

  _____

- If you had the chance to do it all over again, what would you do differently? Why? _____

  _____

  _____

- Write down one thing you didn't do that you wish you had: _____

  _____

- Now, list one thing you can do to ensure the success of your next activity: _____

  _____

9

HOW TO CLEAN A CAMPSITE

APPLYING LEADERSHIP

SISTER PACKER PULLED A BAG of marshmallows from a shopping bag.

"Here you go, Amie," she said, handing the marshmallows to a young woman on the other side of the campfire. "Is this what you wanted?"

Seventeen-year-old Amie Thomas pulled a face, holding the bag between her fingers as if it were a pair of moldy sweat socks.

"Eeeew," she said. "I don't like marshmallows."

A half dozen young women spoke up at once.

"I'll have them!"

"Amie, give them to me!"

"No, me! *Me*! Give them to me!"

Amie scrunched her nose as she looked around the campfire. It was the second night at girls' camp, and so far sweets and treats had been few and far between. The bag of marshmallows had the entire group suddenly hungry.

"I suppose we could share them," Amie said. "Or . . ."

Her eyes flew open as if something incredible had just occurred to her. "No! Wait . . . I've got a better idea!"

She looked around the circle of anxious faces. "Sister Anderson has been asking us to make sure our campsites are all clean, but I've noticed little bits of litter collecting around ours. So how about this: there's a certain piece of litter in the brush. If anyone can find the one I'm thinking about, we'll make s'mores!"

She didn't have to ask twice. The next minute the young women were scouring the campsite, picking up the little bits and pieces of litter that had been collecting over the past couple of days.

As president of the Laurel class, Amie could have demanded that everyone get out there and clean up the camp. She could have assigned someone to do it. She could have kept the chore as a punishment for someone late to breakfast or dinner.

Instead, she turned the chore into a game. With a little creativity, she got the work done without anyone realizing they were working. Not only that, but she probably got the campsite cleaned better too.

As a leader, you're responsible for getting things done. And sometimes the tasks you're given aren't all that much fun. You might get the job done by yelling, shouting, or making threats. But if you're creative, you can often find ways to get the best from everyone without them all hating you for it.

A man named Hal was my boss at an aquatics base one summer, and he had a unique way of getting everyone up in the morning.

"I want to have staff flag ceremony at seven o'clock every morning," he announced at the first of the summer. "You won't get yelled at if you're late, but you *will* have to do kitchen duty for the rest of the day."

You won't get yelled at . . .

Right, I thought. *How's he ever going to get everyone up then?*

But Hal kept his word. He started flag ceremony on the dot of seven every morning. But he never got mad if anyone came late. Instead, he'd smile warmly and say something such as, "Good morning, Bryan! It's good to see you out!"

And then—almost as an afterthought—he'd say, "By the way, while you're washing dishes this morning, would you remind the cook that we need a batch of brownies for Scoutmaster Roundtable?"

Hal didn't yell. He didn't get mad. He didn't pull faces. In fact, he was actually pretty friendly about the whole thing!

But boy, was he effective! People were rarely late. And the whole thing even became kind of fun. On mornings after we'd been up late and it was hard getting out of bed—or when someone's alarm clock went off late—it wasn't unusual to see panic-stricken people streaking through the sagebrush to be on time, many of them still pulling on their uniforms as they ran.

We once had a ninth-grade president at my junior high school who was a genius at applying leadership. Her name was Jordyn. I once watched her conduct a student council meeting the day before a ninth-grade dance.

"Okay," she said, looking around the table. "Remember that the principal didn't want to let us have this dance. We had to fight to get it, so we need to make certain it's *fantastic*!"

She checked her notes. "Sariah, you've got the refreshments all taken care of?"

"Punch and brownies," Sariah replied. "I'm picking them up after school tomorrow."

"And you've got plenty of cups and napkins?"

"My mom took me to buy them last night."

"What about tables?"

Sariah nodded toward a boy on the other side of the table. "Parker's taking care of them for me, right?"

"All set," Parker said.

"Good!" Jordyn turned to another student. "What about decorations? Are you going to be ready?"

"We're good to go," Levi answered. "We've made all the banners, but they're still playing volleyball in class, so we can't actually put anything up in the gym until after school."

"But you have everything you need?"

"Yup. All set and ready to go."

"Do you need any help?"

"I don't think so. But if anyone wants to help, you're welcome to come."

Jordyn put a finger on her cheek. "Is it going to look good? I mean, I hate to ask, but you remember how awful it looked *last* year . . ."

"No worries," Levi replied confidently. "We're gonna rock your socks."

Jordyn smiled. And as she continued with her checks, I realized I was watching a gifted leader. She didn't get after anyone. She didn't embarrass anyone. She didn't pressure anyone.

But with a simple, low-key approach, she reminded everyone how important their roles were and to make certain everyone was ready to go.

Let's take a minute to try something. Get a pen or pencil and—just to get your creative juices flowing—answer the questions in the following activity:

Applying Leadership Discovery

- Think of a great leader you've had. What was his or her name? _____

- Why did you like this leader so much? (Can you think of two or three reasons?) _____

  _____

  _____

- Think of some aspect of his or her leadership style you especially liked or appreciated. What was it?

  _____

  _____

  _____

- Describe how you might use that technique while leading your group: _____

  _____

  _____

All done?

Did you learn anything? Did you come up with any ideas?

Every time I watch a good leader in action, I always come away with new ideas. I change them around to fit my own style and personality, of course, but many of my best, most effective ideas have come from watching other leaders.

I used to coach little league football with a man who was a great coach and an inspired leader. Sometimes we'd be practicing something like snap counts, which can be pretty tricky. A lot of coaches drive the idea home by yelling, screaming, and terrifying their players into doing them right.

Coach Comer's style was different.

At the end of practice, he'd announce, "All right, everyone line up for dirty three hundreds."

Everyone would instantly groan. "Dirty three hundreds" was a brutal conditioning drill everyone hated, and the kids were already worn out from two hard hours of practice.

Coach Comer would act surprised and say, "You don't wanna do 'em? Okay . . . well, if you can pass a snap-count drill, we'll skip the dirty three hundreds."

The players would instantly cheer and line up: a dreaded drill was suddenly an exciting contest.

"On three," the coach would say. "Down! Seeeeet! Hut! Hut!—"

If anyone jumped before the third "hut," the whole team would have to sprint twenty yards and back. And then we'd do it again. Coach Comer would alter the cadence each time, changing the count from three to two and then back to three again, forcing the kids to pay attention. Just like they had to do in an actual game.

And whenever anyone jumped, the coach would just grin like a kid who'd pulled a prank as the kids ran their sprint. He didn't yell, and he didn't make a fuss. He didn't have to. He had changed a brutal drill into an awesome game. He trained his players in a positive way. He got everyone to perform and do their best without anyone hating him or thinking he was an awful tyrant.

But the cleverest thing about Coach Comer's style was that he had the kids believing that running the drill was *their* idea!

And *that* is good leadership.

Everyone approaches leadership differently. And your own style will change and develop as you become more experienced. In time you'll develop a style that fits your own unique talents and personality.

In the meantime, think about great leaders, teachers, and coaches you've had. Is there anything about their styles that might work for you? Did they have any techniques or ideas you could borrow? Give them a try!

Every single technique might not work for you. But that's okay! Start trying things. Make adjustments to ideas that don't exactly fit your style. Throw out ideas that don't work and hang on to those that do!

I was watching a seventh-grade basketball team once. With just minutes to go before tip-off, they only had five players.

Boy, those guys are gonna get tired! I thought.

As a coach, I would have been worried sick if I only had five players at game time. And I couldn't believe how calmly this coach was handling it.

A few minutes after the game started, a sixth boy came running in. And I was curious to see how the coach would react. A lot of coaches, I know, would have ripped the kid apart for being late. But not this one. Instead, he smiled warmly.

"Hi, Chris!" he said, reaching over and patting the boy on the knee. "I was starting to get worried."

Starting to get worried? I would have had my fingernails completely chewed off!

I don't know everything that was going on that night. But the image of that coach greeting a tardy player and making him feel welcome and wanted has always stuck with me.

I learned something about coaching that night. And I remembered it the next time a player of mine was late to a game or a practice.

Have you still got your pencil handy? Let's try another activity. Take a couple of minutes and answer the following questions:

Applying Leadership Activity

- Think of a terrific leader you've worked with. Try to picture this person as clearly as you can. (Can you see your leader's face? Hear his or her voice? Hear him or her laugh?)

- Good! Now, try to picture him or her encouraging someone who's always late to be on time to the next activity. What do you think he or she might say?

  _____

  _____

- How would that leader encourage everyone to be still and quiet during an important lesson? _____

  _____

  _____

- How would he or she encourage the group clown to settle down during a serious activity? _____

  _____

- How would he or she deal with someone who didn't want to participate? _____

  _____

  _____

- How would he or she encourage someone to work a little harder? _____

  _____

- What's the most creative thing you've seen that leader do? Is that something you can try yourself? _____

  _____

All done?

How did it go? If you're like me, you now have another handful of ideas to try out. The key is to actually *try* them! Don't let them sit around and gather dust; put them to work. After all, those simple ideas are partly why you appreciate that leader. And they might become the reason your group appreciates you too!

Start today! Choose one or two ideas that you can try out *right now*. Then get to work!

ACTION STEPS!

- Think of a great leader you've had. Think of something you especially admired or appreciated about him or her and write it here: _____

  _____

  _____

- Think of a way you can use that quality yourself. Write it down: _____

  _____

  _____

- Choose one aspect of your former leader's style that you could try. What is it? _____

  _____

  _____

- Now, come up with a way you can put *that* idea into practice. Describe it here: _____

  _____

  _____

- Go back and read what you just wrote. Resolve to try it at your next meeting or activity!

- Think of some unpleasant task or chore your group has to take care of. (Something like cleaning the campsite, straightening up the classroom, picking up equipment, or putting away the chairs.) Now, think of a fun, creative way to get everyone to pitch in. Write your idea down: _____

    _____

    _____

    _____

- Think of a problem you hate dealing with (such as people coming late, not wearing their uniforms, or being unprepared). Now, think of a positive, motivating way to encourage everyone to do better. (Stuck for an idea? Think back to great leaders you've had. How do you think *they* might have handled that problem?) Write your idea here: _____

    _____

    _____

    _____

    Now . . . be sure to try it!

10

RATTLESNAKES, BEARS, AND SCOUT-EATING TROUT

CONTROLLING THE GROUP

THE SCOUTS HAD JUST RETURNED from the camp swimming pool and were thinking about a trip to the lake.

"You just watch," a Scout named Rhett was saying. "I'm gonna get a canoe and splash that goofy lifeguard till he's soaked!"

"You do and he'll kick you off the lake," his friend Fuzzy answered.

"Nah . . . he likes that kinda stuff—" Rhett stopped dead in his tracks and stared. "What's this?"

"What's what?"

Rhett pointed. An enormous plastic spider was hanging in front of his tent. He looked around and pointed. "Look, you've got one too."

"Hey!" a third Scout shouted. "There's another spider over here!"

The puzzled Scouts quickly inspected the campsite. They found spiders hanging in front of the food box, the supply cabinets, and in front of every tent in camp . . . except one.

"A raccoon tail?" Fuzzy asked. "How come Alex and Simon get a raccoon tail?"

"Look at their tent," Rhett said, catching on. "It's the only one in camp that looks halfway organized."

The Scouts took another look around the campsite. Sure enough, every box and tent marked with a spider was in an incredible state of disaster. Alex and Simon's tent, on the other hand, could have been on the cover of the *Boy Scout Handbook*.

Rhett frowned and then walked to the fire pit, where the senior patrol leader was roasting a marshmallow.

"Hey, Lance," he said. "What do we need to do to get a raccoon tail?"

Lance looked puzzled. "A what?"

"Don't act innocent. We know what you're doing."

"I don't know what you're talking about," Lance said, popping the browned marshmallow into his mouth. He smacked his lips. "But if you're scared of spiders, you might think about cleaning up your tents."

Lance maintained his innocence, but during the weeklong summer camp, the boys returned to camp once or twice a day to find coon tails or spiders dangling in front of their tents. It became a game. Everyone wanted coon tails (don't worry, they weren't real), so they began keeping their tents and camping areas more neatly organized. And since they never knew when Spiderman (the name they gave the mysterious camp inspector) was going to visit, they had to keep the camp clean all the time.

One afternoon, Rhett was late for a merit badge class and didn't have time to straighten up. So he took all the socks, towels, candy bars, and other odds and ends cluttering his tent and stuffed them inside his sleeping bag.

When he returned later, he didn't find a spider. But there wasn't a coon tail either. He thought he'd gotten away with it, but when he unrolled his sleeping bag to go to bed, he found it filled with dozens of tiny plastic spiders.

"You just can't fool this guy," he reported the next morning.

Controlling your group can be one of the most challenging aspects of leadership. After all, you need people to follow your instructions. You need them to listen to your directions. You need them to do what you want them to without making them hate you in the process.

Wow. Tough order, huh?

It can be. But there are tricks effective leaders use for controlling rowdy groups. Are you interested in learning a few? Let me give you a few ideas!

The first time I ever conducted tryouts for a basketball team, sixty-four boys showed up, trying out for just twelve positions. I walked into the gym to find boys shooting around, running lay-ups, scrambling after loose balls, and launching shots from all over the floor.

It was total chaos.

But when it came time to start, I simply blew a whistle and said, "Okay, guys, c'mon in and take a knee."

I couldn't believe what happened. Sixty-four seventh-grade boys instantly dropped what they were doing and ran to where I was standing in center court. The whole bunch of them knelt around me, giving me their complete, total, undivided attention.

At that moment I had absolute control over that energetic bunch of boys. Was that because I was the most fantastic leader on the planet?

No.

Because I'd yelled and shouted?

No.

Because I'd threatened to make them run laps?

Still no!

They were following my directions because I was the key to making the team, and they didn't want to miss out.

There's an important key there. Did you catch it? *They were following directions because they didn't want to miss out!*

The junior high I teach at recently began a new incentive program. Every day each student is given a copy of his or her current grades. If he or she is passing *every* class, they get an extra half hour at lunch to watch movies, play soccer, or choose any one of a dozen other activities.

If they're not passing every class, they spend that half hour in the class they're struggling in, finishing assignments or getting help from the teacher.

Do you think that had any effect on our students' grades? You bet it did! The number of failing students instantly dropped by *hundreds*!

Just like the boys trying out for my basketball team, students weren't working to avoid punishment. They were working because there was a reward involved and because *they didn't want to miss out.*

The exciting thing was that students who typically didn't mind failing a class or two were suddenly working!

Why? Because they wanted that extra half hour at lunch! They wanted extra time to hang out with their friends. They wanted more time to talk and play. They worked harder—some of them working for the first time—to keep from missing out on the fun stuff.

In a perfect world, people would work and perform and follow directions simply because that's the right thing to do. But some members of your group might not be so enlightened. You might need to find ways to motivate them.

The trick is finding the right bait.

I used to run a Cub Scout camp where four hundred boys and leaders showed up every morning, all of them fired up and eager for a day of fun and adventure.

As everyone gathered for our opening ceremony I had to take control and get the attention of those excited, energetic kids. If you've ever been around Scouts, you know they have a special tradition. Whenever you need everyone's attention, you simply put your right hand up and make the Scout sign. Everyone else is supposed to instantly stop talking and do the same thing.

I could have done that, but I wanted to be original. So as those supercharged boys gathered around, I simply began telling stories. I didn't ask for attention, I didn't ask anyone to be quiet, I didn't announce that I was beginning the ceremony. I just started talking.

"There're bears in this canyon," I'd say, talking normally, as if everyone was already quiet and listening carefully. "Lots of 'em. Big, black hairy ones with mouths full of . . ."

I'd gesture, inviting everyone to fill in the missing word: "Teeth!"

"That's right. Long, sharp . . ."

"Teeth!"

"*Hundreds* of nasty, pointy . . ."

"Teeth!"

"That's right!" I'd hold my hands out and curl my fingers. "And on their paws they have enormous . . ."

"Claws!"

And just like that, I not only had everyone's attention, but I had everyone participating too. The boys were drawn into the story, eager to shout out the missing words at the top of their lungs.

My bait?

Just a story. My audience was nine- and ten-year-old boys, so stories about bears, rattlesnakes, and monstrous, Scout-eating fish in the camp pond were all I needed to get their attention.

And by letting them participate in the stories, I channeled their energy in a positive direction. When I finally made my normal announcements, I had the attention of everyone in camp. And I never once had to ask for it.

Now bear stories are great for controlling ten-year-old Cub Scouts. But if you're president of the Laurel class, captain of the volleyball team, or secretary in the Mia Maid presidency, you might need a different approach.

At girls' camp, a leader named Heather had a fun strategy. She gave each of her campers a necklace on which to hang beads they earned by going on hikes, doing service projects, and presenting lessons.

In addition, the campers could earn special "recognition" beads too. Several times

> **If you've ever been fishing, you know that you can't force a fish to take your hook. But if you offer it the right bait, you sure can tempt it!**

a day, Heather would say something such as, "Lexi, thanks so much for helping with lunch today."

And then she'd give the young woman a recognition bead.

Later, she might say, "Courtney, I noticed you picking up litter on the trail this morning. Thanks so much!"

And she'd give Courtney a bead.

That might seem pretty simple, but it worked. Why was her method so effective?

First, she let everyone know how much she appreciated the little things they were doing. She recognized them for their efforts, and she let everyone know she was watching. And—perhaps most important—she instilled a culture of service in the group. The campers quickly caught on and began looking for little ways to help. They weren't just doing it for the beads, they were doing it because that's simply what campers in their ward did!

"The secret is to catch people doing something good," Heather said. "You go out of your way to 'catch' them doing something you appreciate, and then you mention it. It doesn't take long before people catch on. It creates a culture of doing good."

Bear stories for Cub Scouts, beads for campers—the challenge is figuring out what's going to work for *your* group.

Try this: Think of a problem you have in your group. It might be people showing up late, talking during the lesson, or playing around when you need them to be serious.

Can you think of something?

Okay. Now think of a great leader you've had. It might be an adult leader you've known or someone your own age. And then ask yourself, how would *that* person handle the problem you're facing?

Maybe you've actually seen your leader handle that problem (or one like it) before. And if not, use your imagination—how do you *think* he or she would handle it?

Now, do you think that technique would work for you?

Let's expand our experiment a little bit. (You're going to have to slow down as you do this, so if you're in a hurry, you might want to wait till you have a little more time to finish this section.)

Ready?

Okay.

Think about another effective, inspiring leader you've had. (Or use the same one you used a minute ago, if he or she was especially inspiring.) What's the one thing that really stands out in your mind when you think of him or her?

A magnetic personality?

An ability to motivate?

A great sense of humor?

The fact that he or she took a personal interest in you?

Take a moment to get a firm picture in your mind.

Now, go through the list below and decide how your chosen leader would handle each of the following situations. Don't cheat! And don't skip any! Think up an answer to each situation, even if it's something that doesn't apply to you. Answering each question will get your creative juices flowing and condition you to think up solutions when you need them.

So, how would that leader deal with someone who:

- Talks while someone's giving instructions? (Don't read on until you've come up with an answer!)
- Is always late?
- Won't follow directions?
- Won't stay in his or her seat?
- Makes jokes and goofs around when the group needs to be serious?
- Complains about everything?
- Sees the worst in everything?
- Picks on or teases other people?
- Won't put away his or her cell phone?
- Makes rude comments?
- Won't settle down?
- Won't listen?

Wow! That's quite a list! (I hope you never have to deal with all those things!) But if you worked your way through every item, seriously thinking up solutions, you probably came up with some ideas. You began "conditioning" yourself to deal with problems, which will prepare you to handle actual situations when they come up.

And here's something else to think about: someone once told me that if you ask good teachers how they keep control of their classes, most of them won't be able to tell you.

Seriously!

And that's because most effective teachers rarely have discipline problems. Why? It's partly because they keep their students so involved, so busy, and so engaged that the kids never have *time* to mess around.

This is an important lesson. If you take the time to be certain everyone has plenty to do, if you give them compelling, creative activities to keep them busy, they'll be less likely to cause problems.

And that makes things easier for everyone!

Controlling a group is a skill that's essential to good leadership. But it takes practice. So don't get discouraged if it takes a while to get the hang of it. Try things. Ask your advisors and counselors for suggestions. Think of how leaders you know have handled problems similar to yours.

You *will* get better!

And your time and efforts *will* make a difference!

ACTION STEPS!

- Think of a problem you've had to deal with in your group. What was it? _____

_____

- Could you have avoided the problem by having more compelling activities going on? If so, what could you have done to keep the problem from coming up?

_____

_____

_____

- How did you handle the problem? _____

_____

_____

_____

- Did that work? (If not, what could you have done differently?) _____

_____

_____

- Now that you've been through it, how will you handle that same problem if it comes up again?

_____

_____

_____

- Think back to an effective leader you've had. Did that person have certain techniques for dealing with rowdy or inappropriate behavior? Come up with one technique you've seen that seems especially effective and that you might be able to use yourself. What is it? _____

_____

_____

_____

- Think of another technique you've seen in church, school, sports, or some other activity that's been effective. Describe it here: _____

_____

_____

_____

- Is there a way to use that technique in your group? How? _____

_____

_____

- We're going to change directions here, but think of someone in your group who's "challenging" to deal with—someone you constantly have to keep an eye on. (You don't need to write his or her name!)

- What does he or she do that is most distracting to the group? _____

  _____

  _____

- Is there something positive you can have that person do that might keep him or her from goofing around or doing whatever it is that's causing problems? If so, write it here: _____

  _____

  _____

- Come up with three positive things about the person you're thinking about. Write them here (Don't cheat now! Do this!): _____

  _____

  _____

  _____

- The next time your special friend has you on the verge of "melting down," remember those things you just listed! Promise to focus first on his or her positive qualities and not the negative ones!

11

HOW TO TRAIN
A LIFEGUARD
EFFECTIVE TEACHING

EIGHTEEN-YEAR-OLD HEATHER ALLRED placed a ten-dollar bill on the edge of the diving board.

"This is your first bonus," she said to her lifeguarding class. "The first person to swim the length of the pool and back gets it."

"All right!" a confident swimmer exclaimed, flexing her muscles. "That money's mine!"

"In your dreams," one of her friends taunted.

"No prizes for second place!" the first swimmer responded. "Which leaves *you* out!"

Heather just smiled. The aspiring lifeguards were brimming with energy and confidence, just the way good lifeguards should be. But they were about to learn an important lesson.

"There is one condition," Heather announced casually. "To win, you have to finish in less than twenty-five seconds."

The aspiring lifeguards jeered and hooted; it was clear they didn't consider that much of a challenge.

"Okay, then," Heather said, holding up a stopwatch. "On your marks, get seeeeet . . . *go!*"

The swimmers leaped into the pool and began splashing furiously for the far side. To become lifeguards, they had to be powerful swimmers, but within seconds they began to realize there was more to Heather's challenge than they thought.

The thing was, everyone was wearing street clothes over their swimsuits. Heather had allowed them to remove their shoes, but they were all wearing long pants, shirts, and socks. Those clothes not only created drag in the water, but as they became soaked, they also became heavy, making it even harder to swim.

Everyone eventually finished the race, but not within the specified time. And everyone was so exhausted, it was several minutes before they were breathing normally enough for Heather to make her point.

"It never fails," she said, finally. "You all know that you have to remove your street clothes before attempting a water rescue."

She paused to let the message sink in. "But people drown every year because they think the rules don't apply to them. They don't take that extra second to remove clothing that makes it more difficult to swim. But do you now understand *why* it's so critical that you do?"

The aspiring lifeguards were still chuffing for breath. But they nodded respectfully. Heather had made her point so well that everyone understood it perfectly. And she made it in a way no one would ever forget.

As a leader, you'll have opportunities to teach important lessons too. Unfortunately, lectures aren't always high priorities for people your age. After all, teenagers spend loads of time in school, and by the time they get to you, they're ready for something different. So finding ways to present important information can be a challenge.

The good news is that effective teaching isn't impossible. In fact, it can be a lot of fun. Teaching provides opportunities to stretch your imagination and develop your creativity. And when you present a great lesson, you can be sure it'll make a difference in the lives of those you teach.

How do you get started?

Let's take a look.

Give Them a Reason to Learn

The best way to prepare a group for any lesson is to first convince them that it's important.

Let me give you an example.

When I was in high school, my calculus teacher once gave us a page of difficult problems.

"You have twenty minutes," he said, as if giving us all the time in the world.

We worked and struggled for about fifteen minutes. The problems were long and complicated—the kind that made you realize why they're called "problems." And most of us only managed to complete the first three or four.

"What's the matter?" Mr. Birch finally asked. "What's taking you so long?"

"It's hard!" someone exclaimed.

"*Hard*?" The teacher looked at us like we were the biggest bunch of wimps he'd ever taught. But then he smiled. "Would you like to see an easier way?"

Yes!

You see, we *knew* how difficult those problems were. And if there was an easier way, we wanted to know it!

If Mr. Birch had simply started his lecture as usual, many kids wouldn't have given him their full attention. (You go to school; you know how it is!) But by first giving us a challenge—by exposing us to a problem—he prepared us. He gave us a reason to *want* to know more. And believe me, when he finally began his lesson, we gave him our undivided attention.

Remember Heather, the lifeguard I introduced at the beginning of this chapter? To pass first aid, her lifeguards needed to demonstrate the proper way to remove surgical gloves.

"You've gotta be careful," Heather explained, "because if there's blood on them you could expose yourself to an infectious disease."

Yawn . . . nobody cared.

But Heather was prepared for that. She had everyone pull on a pair of disposable gloves. Then—with a knowing grin—she squirted a dab of whipped cream into everyone's gloved hands.

"Okay, then," she said. "I'd like you to take your gloves off . . . without getting any whipped cream on you."

And just like that, a dull lesson was suddenly a game. And no one was able to remove those tight-fitting gloves without making a mess. So when Heather finally demonstrated the proper way to remove them, everyone watched her eagerly. And then they asked for another chance with the whipped cream.

You see, when everyone sees the *need* for your lesson, they'll be more receptive to it. They'll pay better attention. They'll ask better questions, and they might even ask for more.

I have a young friend named Jantzen who used to work for me at Cub Scout camp.

"I'm going to teach you the names of trees and plants today," he once told a group of Scouts. (His announcement was followed by a chorus of moans and groans.) "Then we'll have a contest. We'll see how many you can find."

And just like that, he had everyone's attention. With the promise of a contest, the boys *wanted* to learn. They watched— and listened—as carefully as demolition experts learning to defuse nuclear bombs.

But the most exciting thing happened after Jantzen finished his presentation. As soon as he turned the boys loose, they went tearing around the meadow, identifying every tree and plant in sight—and they were still *learning*! The lesson wasn't over just because Jantzen finished teaching. As the boys raced around, they were honing their skills, asking questions, and putting into practice everything they'd just learned.

Did they feel like they were in school?

No!

Feel like they were learning?

No!

Having fun?

Yes! They were having a *blast*!

The next time you plan a lesson, give your group a *reason* to listen. Invent a game, a contest, an event—anything to give the group a way to use their new skills and a reason to pay attention.

A Laurel class I know once had a lesson in Dutch oven cooking. After the class president, Rian, explained what they were

STEPPING UP, TAKING CHARGE & LEADING THE WAY

going to do, one of the young women asked, "Will we get to make something?"

"Absolutely!" Rian said. "We're going to make peach cobbler." She grinned slyly. "And I've invited the priests to judge them."

Think anyone was sleeping during *that* lesson?

Not a chance! Knowing that the boys were going to be tasting their work, those young women gave Rian their undivided attention!

To ensure a great lesson, give your group a reason to pay attention.

Use Your Creativity

You know better than anyone how much time teenagers spend in school—and that when it's time for your Scout meeting or Young Women activity, they might not want any more. So you have to make your presentation creative enough that it doesn't seem like more school. One way to do that is to present it in a way that's never been done before.

I have a friend named Tucker who's great at this. When he was assigned to teach astronomy at summer camp, he announced that class would be at ten o'clock . . . in the morning.

"Tucker," someone said patiently, "you're supposed to teach astronomy at night."

"I know," he said. "And we'll go out at night. But *class* is in the morning."

I knew Tucker well enough that I was excited to see what he had in mind. And I wasn't disappointed. He had his campers all lying on their backs inside a dark tent.

"This is Scorpio," he said. He placed a flashlight behind a paper plate in which he'd punched holes in the shape of a constellation. Sharp pinholes of light in the shape of Scorpio appeared on the roof of the tent. "Can anyone see the scorpion?"

"I can!"

A boy hopped to his feet and pointed out the scorpion.

"Why's that one star so big?" someone asked from the darkness.

"Because it's huge," Tucker explained. "It's called Antares, and it's like four hundred times bigger than our sun."

I heard a ripple of wows through the tent as the boys tried to imagine something so enormous.

Tucker went through several more constellations, making his presentation interactive by letting everyone participate. And the boys became more and more excited. By the time the lesson was over, they couldn't wait for dark to see everything for real.

The next time you have a lesson to teach, look for a creative way to present it. Let your imagination run wild! You'll not only make your lesson more fun, but chances are you'll have more fun *teaching* it too.

Introduce the Element of Challenge

Challenge?

Sure! Try adding something unexpected to the mix, just to make things more exciting. If you're building fires, for instance, try using damp wood. If you're tying knots, have everyone do it wearing gloves or with just one hand—or maybe even blind-folded! And if you're teaching scriptures, find unusual ways to apply them to events happening in the lives of your group.

Adding a degree of challenge to your lesson makes it less ordinary. It makes it more exciting, more adventurous, and more fun!

This is silly, but I was teaching three-digit multiplication to a class of seventh graders one day. You know, problems like this:

$$\begin{array}{r} 468 \\ \times\ 532 \\ \hline \end{array}$$

What a snooze!

The kids weren't interested, my student aide wasn't interested—*I* wasn't even interested!

But out of the blue I asked, "Think you could do one holding your breath?"

Eyes that had been glazing over suddenly came back to life. I wrote a problem on the board, holding a notebook over it so no one could see it.

"Everybody ready?"

Heads bobbed enthusiastically.

"Okay, then . . . ready, set, go!"

It sounded like a roomful of vacuum cleaners as thirty-eight students inhaled together. Their cheeks puffed out like squirrels preparing for winter as they began scribbling.

Like I said, it was silly. But a dull subject was suddenly fun. And you know what happened next? As soon as we were done, the kids asked for another one!

Five minutes earlier I had a roomful of students lapsing into comas. But now they were actually *asking* for more! They wanted more *math*!

("I can just hear it now," I told them. "You're all gonna go home and say, 'My teacher's so mean he doesn't even let us breathe!' ")

That's what the element of challenge can do to an ordinary lesson!

Use Your Resources

Remember Tucker, the character who taught astronomy first thing in the morning? I ran into him at the camp rifle range one time when I knew he was supposed to be teaching.

"Where's your class?" I asked.

"Oh, I'm not teaching it this week."

"Really? Why not?"

"We've got an astronomy professor in camp. The guy writes *books* about stars. So he's teaching my class for me."

"Wow. You really let him do that?"

Tucker gave me his most patient expression. "The guy knows every star in the sky *and* its little sister. I'd be crazy *not* to let him."

Well, he had a point. And it's something to keep in mind. If you're scheduled to teach first aid and someone's mother is a nurse, ask her to help. If you're teaching drama and Tallie's the star of the local Shakespearean club, turn the stage over to her!

There are times when you'll want the spotlight all to yourself. But if someone in the group has the skills to teach a particular lesson, why not let them? If it's a special talent of theirs, they might have insights that wouldn't occur to you. Besides, giving others a chance to share the limelight is always a good idea.

Use your resources! Let others help as much as possible.

Spark their interest. Give everyone a reason to learn!

Add the element of challenge to your presentation.

Be creative! Present your lesson in a way they've never seen before.

Teaching your peers can be one of the most exciting, most rewarding aspects of leadership. So make the most of your opportunities. Learn to stretch your imagination. Use your creativity. And make your next presentation the most fantastic one you've ever taught!

ACTION STEPS!

- Think of the next lesson you're scheduled to teach. How can you get everyone involved right from the start? _____

_____

_____

- Is there an object lesson you can use to heighten interest? (Think hard now!) Describe it here:

_____

_____

_____

- Come up with an activity or contest for everyone to practice the skills you want to teach: _____

_____

_____

_____

- Is there a new, creative, or unusual way to present your lesson? (Maybe something no one's seen or thought of before?) What is it? _____

_____

_____

_____

- Is there an element of challenge you can add to make things even more interesting? What is it?

_____

_____

_____

- Look through your resource sheets. Are there people in the group who could help or even teach the lesson on their own? Is there someone who could share a personal experience? Choose one person who can help contribute. Write his or her name and how you can use him or her: _____

_____

12 TEACHERS, CREATURES, AND OTHER TEENAGE CHALLENGES

EFFECTIVE COUNSELING

JENNIE KOFFORD'S FACE was as red as an overripe cherry.

"Ooh!" she squealed, slamming her books down on a desk. "I hate Mr. Rivers! I just *hate* him!"

I jumped at my desk, startled by Jennie's outburst. A vibrant, animated ninth-grader, Jennie had the personality of a firecracker. Besides being a terrific student, she was a talented actress and could sing like everyone's favorite contestant on *American Idol*.

But I had never seen her angry.

"What's wrong?" I asked.

She whirled around so fast that I automatically leaned back in my chair: if her eyes could have fired laser beams, she would have vaporized me on the spot.

"Teachers!" she exclaimed, as if that explained everything.

"Teachers?"

"They're the worst!"

"They're not all bad," I offered weakly.

"Mr. Rivers!" she exclaimed. "Do you know what he did?"

"Why don't you tell me?"

"The elementary schools are all coming here tomorrow. We're doing a matinee of *Beauty and the Beast*."

I nodded. Jennie had a role in the play. I hadn't seen it yet, but I'd heard she was fantastic.

She held her hands out as if the problem was obvious.

"There's a choir festival tomorrow!" she said. "And Mr. Rivers won't let me skip it for the play!"

Ah. The pieces fell into place. Mr. Rivers was the school's brilliant (but eccentric) chorus teacher. There was a conflict between the play and the choir festival, and Mr. Rivers wasn't going to be reasonable about it.

"Can you believe that? There are like forty girls in the chorus. They'll never even *miss* me! But who's going to take my part in the play?"

"Wow," I said. "He really won't let you miss the festival?"

"No!"

"Are you singing a solo or something?"

"No! Nothing! I'm just another face in the crowd! If I'm not there, no one will even know the difference!"

"Hmmmm." I shook my head. It did sound pretty unfair. "What about your drama teacher? What did he say?"

"Oh, he's furious! But what can he do?"

I shook my head again. The truth was, I'd had run-ins with the chorus teacher myself. But I didn't want to say that. I didn't know all the facts, and I didn't want to make Jennie's situation worse by saying the wrong thing.

Instead, I went and sat next to her as she vented her frustration. As she talked, her temper cooled. And it wasn't long before she was fairly calm again. When another student walked in, Jennie turned and (with a smile) said, "You wanna guess what Mr. Rivers did this time?"

And then she repeated her story. But this time there was a joking tone in her voice, as if the situation had suddenly become funny. When the bell rang for everyone to go to class, Jennie came up and smiled.

"Thanks, Mr. B."

"For what?"

"For letting me vent."

"Not a problem. You'll let me know what happens?"

"You can count on it!"

In the end, the disputing teachers worked out some sort of arrangement that made everyone happy. But that's not the point. For a while, Jennie was like a pressure cooker—boiling over and ready to explode. She needed a chance to vent her frustrations, and I felt good that she'd come to me.

Because you're a leader, people will sometimes come to you with problems too. Sometimes—like Jennie—they'll just need someone to listen to their frustrations. Other times they might have deeper, more significant problems to work out.

Whatever the case, you need to be sure that you respond appropriately. Offering a listening ear can be a great help to someone who's hurting. At the same time, you're not a trained therapist. You need to be sure that you don't do more harm than good.

So when your turn comes, keep these tips in mind:

Be a Good Listener

When Jennie came to talk with me, she wasn't looking for advice. She didn't need to hear about my experiences with the goofy chorus teacher. Instead, she needed a chance to share *her* feelings. She needed someone who could listen sympathetically to *her* frustrations.

Many people are like that. They might be feeling hurt or disappointed by something. Or maybe they're having a bad day. They might just need a chance to talk and to have someone who is willing to listen.

So let them talk! Don't interrupt with opinions or stories of your own. Instead, let them have the stage. Give them a chance to get it all out.

Be an Active Listener

Even though you're not doing the talking, you can still be part of the conversation. Let your friend know you're listening by asking questions such as, "What did you do then?" or "How did that make you feel?" or "Why do you think she did that?"

Simple questions like these will assure your friend that you're paying attention and that you're interested. And they'll encourage your friend to keep talking.

As you listen, it's important to avoid seeming distracted. Put away your cell phone. Don't look at the clock. Instead, keep your eyes on your friend. Nod once in a while. Really focus on what they're saying. Try to understand what they're feeling.

Remember that your friend is hurting and has come to you for help. That deserves your full attention.

Remain Neutral

When a friend has a problem, it's easy to get caught up in things. But keep in mind that you don't know all the facts and that you're only hearing one side of the story. Be careful not to inflame an emotional situation with comments like, "I can't believe she did that!" or, "He's such a jerk!"

Instead, try to remain neutral. Use milder, less inflammatory comments such as, "That must have been really embarrassing," or "How did you feel about that?"

People rarely think clearly when they're angry or emotional. And by remaining neutral, you become a calming influence. You help to defuse the emotion and allow your friend to calm down to a point where he or she can make better decisions.

Avoid Giving Advice

When someone's struggling, it's natural to want to help. It's easy to start offering advice and making suggestions.

But remember that you don't know all the facts. You're not a therapist. And what might be right for you might not be the best choice for someone else. So as tough as it is, it's best to avoid giving advice.

Remember Jennie, the young woman I introduced at the beginning of this chapter? In her situation, I might have simply defied my chorus teacher and performed in the play. (After all, who's he to tell *me* what to do!) But that probably would have made things even worse, and I'm glad I didn't suggest it to Jennie.

Instead, by simply giving her an outlet for her frustrations, I allowed her to calm down. And she was then able to find a better solution by herself. The most helpful thing I did was simply listen.

There may be times, of course, when a problem is so bad that someone needs professional counseling. And then it's appropriate to suggest visiting with a parent, teacher, counselor, or church leader. After all, such professionals are trained to deal with tough problems, and they have experience at it.

I once had a student named Michelle in my ninth-grade geometry class. She was the most lively, energetic student I had. So when she spent half the period with her eyes closed and her head bent over her desk one day, I asked if anything was wrong.

She stared at me blankly. "Yeah. I had to have two teeth pulled this morning. And the shots are starting to wear off."

"Ouch. You gonna be okay?"

"Yeah. I'll be okay."

The next period, though, I was just finishing a lesson when I looked up to see Michelle in the doorway. She was waving frantically.

"What's the matter?"

"The shots wore off," she said, bouncing up and down, trying to relieve the pain. Her face was pale and tears were rolling down her cheeks. "And I hurt! I hurt so bad I can't stand it!"

"Didn't the dentist give you any painkillers?"

"Yes! But my dad doesn't want me to take them. I tried to call him, but he's not at work. And I can't find my mom."

"Okay," I said. "What do you need me to do?"

The tears rushed down her face. "I hurt so bad I can't think. I need somebody to tell me what to do!"

Michelle was in such pain that I hurt just watching her. But I knew what to do. I knew one of Michelle's uncles. We called him, and he was able to take her back to the dentist.

Most times, being a good listener is the best thing you can do for a friend with a problem. But if the situation is ever critical—if there's ever any kind of danger involved—don't hesitate. Notify a parent, teacher, coach, or church leader right away.

Like many things, counseling is a skill you can improve with practice. So let's take a few minutes to try something. Get a pencil and try the counseling discovery on the next two pages. (It's not a test, so just relax and answer the questions the best you can!)

EFFECTIVE COUNSELING DISCOVERY

1. Picture one of your good friends. Write his or her name here:

_____

_____

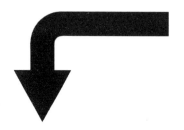

2. How would you know if he or she was having a bad day or was worried about some problem? (How would he or she look? How would he or she act?)

_____

_____

_____

3. What could you say—in a friendly, nonthreatening way—that could let your friend know you'd listen if he or she wanted to talk about the problem?

_____

_____

_____

8. What could you do later to show your friend that you care, that you support him or her, and that you're still thinking of him or her?

_____

_____

_____

7. Suppose something comes up and your friend has to leave before he or she is done talking. What could you say before he or she leaves?

_____

_____

6. List two things you could say to encourage him or her to keep talking:

_____

_____

_____

5. What could you say to show that you understand what your friend is saying?

_____

_____

4. Think of three things you could do or say as your friend talks to show that you're really listening:

_____

_____

_____

Okay, how'd that go?

Answering those questions should have given you a couple of ideas for counseling a friend with a problem. I hope those problems are never serious, but you should now be better prepared for whatever comes up.

In the meantime, there's one more thing to keep in mind:

Watch for People Who Need to Talk

You might be willing to ask for help when you need it, but not everyone is. That means you should watch for people who might need a helping hand or a listening ear but who are hesitant or embarrassed to ask.

I was helping a student after school one day when a young man named James walked in and sat by the window. That wasn't unusual (he used my window to watch for his mother), but I could tell something was wrong.

For one thing, he wasn't smiling (he usually smiled so much I actually called him "Smilin' Jim"). He wasn't talkative (he usually chattered like a squirrel with a sugar rush). And he didn't even say "hi" when he walked in (he rarely walked past my room without poking his head in the door for a quick wave).

So as soon as I had a second I walked over to sit by him.

"How was your day?"

"Okay."

"Doing anything fun tonight?"

"Not really."

"Sit by any girls today?"

"Not really."

Wow, I thought, *I made a comment about girls, and he didn't even flinch: things are even worse than I thought!*

I finally just asked, "Everything okay?"

"Yeah . . ."

"Hey, James," I said. "It's me. What's going on?"

He looked out the window for another moment and then shrugged. "I might not pass English this term."

"Really?"

"Yeah. If I don't, I won't be able to play football . . . *and* I'll have to take summer school."

"Ouch . . . have you talked to your teacher about it?"

"I was going to. But he's busy."

"Hmmmm. Is there anything you can do to bring your grade up?"

"Well, I've got some worksheets. But I don't know how to do them."

I felt like the sun had just come out. "What if someone was able to help you? Would you be interested?"

"I guess so."

It just so happens that I used to teach English. James and I spent the next hour completing worksheets, and he did so well that he was able to retake a test the next morning that raised his grade to a B.

And just like that, Smilin' Jim was back in business.

I knew there was something wrong the moment James walked into my classroom. But without a little prompting, he wouldn't have asked for help. So if I hadn't reached out, he might have ended up with an F in English, missed out on football, and wound up in summer school too.

Whether you're a leader or not, you can keep an eye out for people who seem down, unhappy, or out of sorts. You don't need to wait for such people to come to you. If you sense something is wrong, go ahead and ask that person to go for a walk. Give him or her a chance to talk. You don't need to force your friend, but if you give him or her an opportunity to open up, it might happen.

And then be ready to listen.

As an effective leader, you can be a tremendous help when someone's struggling with a problem. By offering a listening ear, by showing that you care, and by checking up on your friend from time to time, the two of you will grow closer. You'll forge a bond of friendship, respect, and gratitude that will last a lifetime!

ACTION STEPS!

- Practice good listening. Find a friend or family member right now and encourage him or her to talk.

Ask that person about his or her day or something he or she has been doing. Then *listen*. Ask questions. But practice letting your friend do all the talking.

- Describe how it went. Was it hard to keep that person talking? Were you able to ask questions that encouraged that individual? Was it difficult focusing on what he or she was saying? Write your reflections here: _____

  _____

  _____

- Think of a time someone told you about a bad day or shared some other problem. On a scale of 1 to 10, how well did you really *listen*? Circle a number:

  1   2   3   4   5   6   7   8   9   10

- What could you have done better? _____

  _____

  _____

- Think of a time you've been sad, discouraged, or frustrated. Describe it here: _____

  _____

  _____

- Did you talk with anyone about it? If so, how did that feel? (If you didn't, do you think it would have helped?) _____

  _____

- Imagine a friend telling you that he has just been grounded and that he hates his parents. What do you think a good response would be? _____

  _____

- Has there ever been a time when someone has gotten you to open up when you didn't want to talk? How did he or she do that? _____

_____

_____

- Imagine that a friend is worried or bothered about something but doesn't want to talk. How could you encourage her to open up? (Or let her know you're there if she needs you?) _____

_____

_____

13 ▸ FLYING COWS AND THE ENERGIZER BUNNY

GENERATING ENTHUSIASM

JUSTIN PACKER SOARED off the jump, reaching down to grab the edge of his snowboard as he became airborne. He flew through the air like an Olympic medal winner before hitting the slope in a spray of powder. Unfortunately, he was going too fast, and his snowboard spit out from beneath him.

A shrill scream split the air as he snowballed down the slope.

"Aaaaaaaaiiigh!"

Trying not to laugh, I raced down the hill, braking to a stop and spraying him with snow.

"Frosty the Snowdude!" I said. "You okay?"

Justin threw a snowball at me. He was completely covered with snow, his face flushed from the cold. But he was grinning like a little kid on Christmas morning.

"That was gnarly!" he said. "We *have* to do it again!"

"Which part? The jump or the wipeout?"

He smacked me with another snowball and then hopped back onto his board. "You wanna race?"

"Anytime, anywhere."

"Okay, then . . . on your mark, get seeet . . ."

Without waiting for "go!" he took off, shooting down the hill like a kid fleeing Bigfoot.

I raced after him, relishing the cold air on my face and the fresh snow beneath my board.

Justin was one of my best friends. We worked together at summer camp, and we often went snowboarding in the winter. No matter where we were or what we were doing, Justin always reminded me of a can of pop: full of fizz and ready to explode with energy. He was so enthusiastic about life that you couldn't be within a mile of him without catching it yourself.

One time—at Scout Camp—we took a troop of Scouts on an overnight hike. The only thing was that it had been raining all day and the storm didn't show any signs of letting up.

A problem?

Not with Justin along!

The instant we hit the muddy trail, he began leading everyone in a goofy song about a cross-eyed bear. After eight or nine hilarious verses, he launched into a ridiculous story about a flying cow that had the whole troop howling with laughter. He pumped those kids so full of punch and energy that most of them didn't even realize how wet and muddy they were.

A five-mile hike in a rainstorm could have been a miserable experience. But with Justin along, it was an exciting adventure, and—for me—it was one of the highlights of the whole summer.

You probably know people like Justin. People who are always smiling. People who have the energy and enthusiasm to fire up their friends. People who don't complain when the weather is bad or when things go against them. People who can make things better for everyone around them.

People who are fun to be around.

I call these people Battery Chargers. They not only bring out the best in others, but they also help other people become Battery Chargers themselves. Like human whirlwinds, they sweep into their work and energize everyone around them with excitement and enthusiasm.

One of the smartest things you can ever do as a leader is to keep a couple of Battery Chargers around you all the time.

I was teaching a geometry class one day. We were learning proofs, which—if you've ever taken geometry—aren't normally a lot of fun. Everyone's eyes were glazing over, and I was feeling pretty drained myself.

But as I looked around the room, I locked eyes with a young woman named Amanda. She looked at me with the kind of grin kids have when they're thinking, *I know something youuuuuu don't . . .*

Her expression was so silly I began to laugh.

The rest of the class instantly looked up as if wondering, "What's he laughing at? What'd I just miss?"

I looked back at Amanda, and she crossed her eyes.

I was laughing so hard now I had to take a second to catch my breath. And the whole class was looking around and wondering what in the world was so funny.

And that fast, the mood of the whole room changed. I charged back into my lesson like a hungry Scout into a pepperoni pizza. And just like that, geometry was fun again.

All because of the actions of one dynamic person.

And you see, that's why you want Battery Chargers in your group. They keep people happy, cheerful, and optimistic, even when the day is long and the work is hard.

The thing is, *you* can do the same thing yourself. You can put a million-dollar smile on your face first thing every morning and leave it there all day. You can supply the mental boost everyone needs when there's one more hill to climb, one more project to complete, or one more meeting to attend.

Yes, it may seem awkward at first, but if you go out with the attitude that you're going to be enthusiastic, you can be.

How do you do that?

Good question. Start by trying something for me. First, stand up. (Don't just read this, now, do it! Stand up right now!) Shake your arms and stretch a little bit. Take a couple of deep breaths.

Now, smile as big as you can. Bigger . . . *bigger* . . . biiiiiig-ger . . . okay! And now—keeping that huge smile on your face—march around the room. Don't just walk, *march*!

Keep going!

Now, how do you feel? I bet you feel *tons* better than you did two minutes ago. Even if you were already feeling fantastic, I bet you feel even better now.

Why?

Because your brain takes cues from your body. And huge, ear-to-ear grins are signs of happiness. Marching is a sign of energy. So when you're smiling and marching and doing things that happy, energetic people do, your brain starts thinking, *Wow! I don't know what's going on, but I must be happy!*

I know that sounds silly, but it worked, didn't it?

And if you ever need a shot of enthusiasm before a meeting, a talk, or something else that requires an energetic attitude, take a moment to repeat that exercise!

I was teaching school one day, feeling like my batteries were completely drained. My toughest, most challenging class had just left, and I didn't think I had another smidgen of energy left in me.

But then a young woman named Alexis walked in. She smiled, waved, and said, "Hi, Mr. Barker! Are you having a good day?"

At that moment, I remembered that the students filing into the room deserved a fantastic teacher and that I had about two minutes to somehow recharge my batteries for them.

I looked around and spotted Taylor, a boy who usually spends the period bouncing off the walls. He was always bursting with energy, and I knew he could spare a little.

"Hey, Taylor!" I said. "Do me a favor and go out in the hall for a minute."

Taylor looked up in surprise, but dutifully trooped out of the room. I looked around, pointed toward a couple more students, and said, "Would you guys go outside with Taylor?"

I followed the boys out of the room and led them to the bottom of the stairs.

"Okay," I said finally. "I'm racing you up the stairs. Anyone who beats me doesn't have to do his homework tonight. Taylor, you get to say when."

The boys were instantly enthusiastic.

"On three," Taylor announced. "One, two, *three*!"

The next instant, we were flying up the stairs two at a time. I didn't win. (Boy, some of those kids are fast!) But when I marched back into the room (yes, I was marching!), my heart was pounding, I was smiling (it was a real smile too!), and I felt *fantastic*!

Five minutes earlier, my energy level was eighty points below zero. But now? I could have outsmiled the Energizer Bunny.

Yes, it was silly. But it worked!

And it can work for you too.

Let's try something. Get a pencil and try the treasure hunt on the next two pages. We've done these before, so you know the drill. Just relax and answer the questions the best you can.

Are you ready?

Go for it!

Okay . . . how did that go?

If you took the time to fill in the blanks, you now have a few ideas and insights for raising your own energy level and for boosting the enthusiasm of others. That'll get you started. But generating enthusiasm is so important that I've got a few more tips.

First, anytime you need a quick shot of energy or enthusiasm, just put that smile back on your face. March around the room for a minute, race a friend up the stairs, whatever. Just do something to get the sparks flying and the blood pumping.

Second, resolve to *act* happy! If you're always full of gloom and doom—always whining about this and that—people will avoid you like the plague. But when you act happy, upbeat, optimistic, and energetic, you'll draw people in like a magnet. They'll enjoy your company because you'll make them feel good too. You'll help them to recharge their own batteries.

Think about it. Who would *you* rather spend time with? Someone who moans and groans and complains about every little thing in his or her life? Or someone who makes you smile, laugh, and feel good?

You see, people like to laugh. And they like to be happy. So do what it takes to be the bright spot in the life of everyone around you.

ENTHUSIASM TREASURE HUNT

1. Think of the most optimistic, energetic, enthusiastic person you know. Write his or her name here:

_____

_____

2. Describe how you feel when you're around him or her:

_____

_____

_____

3. Think of one quality he or she has that you'd like people to see in you. Write it here:

_____

_____

_____

8. What's something you could do today to develop that quality yourself?

_____

_____

_____

Now . . . go do it!

7. What exactly does he or she do that makes him or her such an effective "Battery Charger"?

_____

_____

_____

6. Suppose you were having an awful, terrible, super-crummy day. Who's one person who would cheer you up just being around him or her?

_____

_____

_____

5. List three things you could do today to develop that quality:

_____

_____

_____

4. Describe why you'd like to have that particular quality:

_____

_____

_____

Third, find a Battery Charger of your own and keep him or her close! Especially if you've got a tough job or chore to take care of. Use that energy to keep the whole group on track.

I once ran the rifle range at a local Scout camp. Take a second to picture that! We had fourteen firing positions on our range, which meant I had to keep an eye on fourteen teenage boys at a time—all of them holding loaded rifles!

You want to talk about stress?

That was stress!

Anyway, the first thing I did that summer was find the happiest, most smiley, cheerful, bright-eyed people on staff and hire them to be my assistants.

And what a difference it made!

I had one assistant named Travis who could have made a hummingbird seem lazy. Most people, for instance, talk . . . like . . . this.

ButTravistalkedlikethis.

He was a teenage speed blur, darting around and bouncing off the walls like the world was his personal pinball machine.

One time, I was feeling a little tense and on edge, so I walked over to where Travis was bobbing his head in rhythm with some song he was humming.

"Travis, tell me a joke."

He didn't hesitate.

"Whydoelephantsfloatontheirbacks? Huh? Doyouknow? Huh? Huh?"

I didn't even have to hear the answer: I was already laughing! But I shook my head and asked, "No, why *do* elephants float on their backs?"

"Sotheseagullshaveanavelbase! Getit? Getit?" He pointed toward his stomach. "A *navel* base!"

Brother.

Another time I looked over to see John, the camp waterfront director, sitting on our bench, watching us as we worked.

"What's going on?" I asked.

"Oh, nothing," he said. "I'm just having a bad day."

And then, before I could respond, he added, "I don't know what it is, but you guys always make me feel good. Being around you guys always cheers me up."

You see?

A couple of good Battery Chargers will do wonders in keeping the whole group happy and focused.

Fourth, resolve now to never complain again. No matter what you're assigned to do, no matter how hot the day is, no matter how awful the job is, just *put a smile on your face and get it done!* Never let *anyone* in your group hear you complain, whine, moan, or groan.

Fifth, look for the best in everything. Not every job you do will be fun. Not every person you work with will be fun. But there's bound to be some good in the situation. So find it! As you do, you'll have more fun. You'll have more success. You'll find adventure around every corner.

Most important, you'll work magic—you'll work *miracles*—in the lives of those you lead.

Don't wait another second!

Go for it!

ACTION STEPS!

- Think of the last activity you took part in. On a scale of 1 to 10, how enthusiastic were you? Circle a number:

  1   2   3   4   5   6   7   8   9   10

- Is there anything you could have done to be more energetic, enthusiastic, or optimistic? What is it?

  _____

  _____

  _____

- Look at the chart below. If the most dynamic, energetic, optimistic Battery Charger you know is at one end, and the world's most deadbeat Battery

Drainer at the other, where would you rank yourself? Actually make a mark on the line (and you can't put yourself right in the middle):

```
ULTIMATE                        ULTIMATE
BATTERY                         BATTERY
DRAINER                         CHARGER
├──────────────── 0 ────────────────┤
```

- Now list three things you could do *today* to move yourself farther down the line:

  1.
  2.
  3.

- Think of someone you know who's full of energy and excitement. What's one thing you especially admire about that person? _____

  _____

- What's something you could do today to develop that quality yourself? _____

  _____

  _____

- Suppose you were assigned a job or activity that didn't seem like a lot of fun. How would the person you listed above deal with the situation? _____

  _____

  _____

- What can you do to help inspire and motivate everyone else to do their best? _____

  _____

  _____

- Think of an activity that fires you up. It might be listening to energetic music, watching a fast game of basketball, or taking a jog around the block. What is it? _____

  _____

  _____

  Now use it the next time you need a quick shot of energy.

ABOUT THE AUTHOR

SHANE BARKER has been working with young people all his life, both as a junior high school math teacher and as the director of Boy Scout camps and high adventure bases. He has served on the faculty of National Camping School and has conducted week-long leadership courses. An avid skier and snowboarder, Barker is an active member of the National Ski Patrol. He is a licensed pilot, a certified scuba diver, and a qualified EMT.

A popular speaker at firesides and youth conferences, Barker is the author of several books for young people. He served a mission to Japan for The Church of Jesus Christ of Latter-day Saints and later graduated from Brigham Young University. He lives in Orem, Utah.

NOTES

SHANE BARKER

_____

_____

_____

_____

_____

_____

_____

_____

_____

_____

_____

_____

_____

_____

_____

_____

                          _____

                          _____

                          _____

                          _____

                          _____

0 26575 55034 4